The Shin

The Elfin Spirits that Guide You According to Your Birth Date and the Evolutionary Lessons They Offer

By The Silver Elves

The Silver Elves

Copyright © 2013 by The Silver Elves, Michael J. Love and Martha C. Love.

ISBN-13:9781494337643
ISBN-10:1494337649

Printed in the United States of America by CreateSpace

Without limiting the rights under the copyright reserved above, no part of this publication may be reproduced, stored in or introduced into a retrieval system, or transmitted in any form or by any means (electronic, mechanical, by photocopying, recording or otherwise) without the prior written permission of the copyright owner and the publisher of the book.

Dedication

THIS BOOK IS DEDICATED TO THE SHINING ONES WHO ARE OUR BENEFACTORS, MENTORS AND KIN.

THE SHINING ONES ARE SURELY GREATER THAN US, MORE POWERFUL AND MORE EVOLVED AND YET IN THE END THEY ARE STILL FAMILY AND THAT IS MORE IMPORTANT THAN ANYTHING.

FROM OUR BIRTH TO OUR DEATH, THEY GUIDE US AND EVERY CHOICE WE MAKE IS ANOTHER LESSON OF LIFE AND MAGIC.

FROM OUR DEATH TO OUR BIRTH, THEY CARRY US, LIKE A WAVE WASHING US TO SHORE AND A NEW INCARNATION.

TABLE OF CONTENTS

Introduction 7

Month: January 13
Month: February 37
Month: March 59
Month: April 83
Month: May 107
Month: June 127
Month: July 149
Month: August 171
Month: September 193
Month: October 215
Month: November 237
Month: December 259

About the Authors 281

INTRODUCTION

The spirits in this book, or Shining Ones as we sometimes call them, are the planetary guardians and evolutionary agents of the Great Magic of Faerie and have authority over various areas of the planet but also over those born on a particular day or time. Many think of the Shining Ones in the way that they view Guardian Angels assuming there is one angel that watches and guides them and only them for their entire life. We elves find this point of view rather egocentric. Even though we elfin have a sense of being royalty, we don't consider ours'elves so important that the Divine would assign a being who is far more evolved and more powerful than us just to guide us individually; although we don't deny the fact that some individuals do have private tutors. Perhaps you are one of them.

Most of us, however, until we have risen higher on the evolutionary ladder of development tend to be in classes with others on our level. This does not preclude the idea of private tutoring or that as we evolve we may apprentice to a Shining One on a more one to one basis, but even in this event the Shining One usually has more than one apprentice.

The Shining Ones don't really guide our lives individually but rather offer us lessons in magic and evolution as individuals, which is to say they have many students but tailor their teaching to the needs, aspirations and visions of each student. They are teachers who offer instruction and the courses you are offered are based in part on the day you were born, the period of the month and the month you were born in. Or really, you were born on a certain day because you are assigned to a certain required course.

Like all education, no one is going to, or can, force you to learn the information offered, and you are free if you desire to contact other teachers and pursue the courses they offer. Still, you should know that the day you are born on represents the essential lesson this spirit offers for this lifetime and if you don't master that course or pursue it the best you can you are missing something essential at this time to your evolutionary education. Under such circumstances it is usually folly to seek other instruction, although you are surely free to do so, but know that the course offered by your natal or birth spirit is a fundamental lesson that you must master to proceed in your evolutionary education.

Still, you are always free to seek other teachers, and most elfin, like most students in elementary, high school and college take or study more than one course or subject at a time. Note, that as an analogy, these courses for the elven are for the most part on the level of college, masters and doctorate levels of evolutionary development.

LEVELS OF DEVELOPMENT

Alas, we simply couldn't write everything about each spirit and what they teach. It would simply have made the book too long. However, with effective and creative use of the elements associated with the spirit, the constellation, the planetary association, the faerie assistants and so on, one may intuit much that is not written out.

Supplementing this book with other books can give one a more expanded view of one's destiny, fate and karma in this lifetime and the evolutionary challenges that confront one. We recommend Monica Buonfiglio's *Cabalistic Angels* in this regard. Knowing one's astrological charts, both natal and progressed, can also be very helpful. If you know the degrees of your Sun, Moon and the planets, you may find our book *An Elven Book of Dreams* as an effective supplement, and Dane Rudhyar's *An Astrological Mandala* is highly recommended. Each of these will provide further understanding concerning your life task and the way to spiritual progress in this lifetime.

COURSE LEVELS

Different individuals, according to their level of evolutionary development, will react to these Shining Ones and the courses they offer in various ways and these have a propensity to come in three basic types:

Evolution 101 Beginners: Undergraduate

Those who are at the beginning of instruction sometimes find that they can't relate to a particular course at all or find it very difficult. They often struggle with the course. Remember, the description given concerns what the spirit offers and is not really about you specifically but the general type that is assigned to this course. It is important to use your intuition when interpreting the description.

Advanced: Masters

Those who are more advanced can relate to the course and even have a certain degree of skill in the magical power already developed but still find that they struggle with it sometimes. These have contented thems'elves with mastering this lesson and no long fight it, although as we say it probably will still provide a challenge for them.

Adept: Doctoral Candidates

The adept have mastered this lesson or are very close to doing so and they are often eager to move on to other studies, which they will surely do in the next lifetime, although like everyone they are free to take whatever "electives" they wish along with these required courses. These individuals are merely refining what they have mastered, putting their own spin on the work, and putting on the finishing touches. These elfin are at a stage where they may teach the course in the future.

Pass/Fail

You should know that in Magic, and in evolutionary matters, action and effort are ultimately everything. You do not have to master the course to pass it, which is to say, move on to another course. You merely have to have a basic understanding and a simple mastery. Some may wish to become great adepts in a particular field that is offered, but no one is required to do so.

The only way you can fail the course is to refuse to put any effort toward its realization. Since these are required courses for your particular evolution, you will, sooner or later, have to pass the course. Although, you are always free to change your major, so to speak. However, that would mean a change of life direction and if you are already on your true course, it would be unlikely that you'd wish to do that.

Associations

You can, as we said, evoke other spirits in this book besides the ones you directly come under. In this way, this book may be thought of as a companion to our *Elven Book of Spirits*. When seeking the assistance of other spirits, however, you should consider the lines and protocols of connection. You could go directly to a particular Shining One; however, it is more effective if you are in some way already linked or associated with them, just as if you are looking for a job you may go to someone in your family or a friend who knows someone in the field, etc. The old saying: *it's not what you know but who you know* is relevant here. Connections ease the way.

There are some spirits that teach similar lessons, so these are linked. But you can also consider that spirits that have the same planetary association as the spirit you were born under, of the spirit of the month you were born in, or the spirit of the period of the month, is directly connected to you. Thus if your teacher is associated with Mars you automatically have a direct connection to other instructors aligned with that planet. This is also true of the constellations, powers, and faerie assistants. Therefore, if your teacher has the Cauldron of Rebirth as a magical power you are connected directly to all others with that power. Of course, the more of these links between the spirits the stronger the connection.

Faerie Assistants

Alas, we couldn't explain the nature of all the faerie assistants without making the book too large and in some cases you may have to do a little research, but keep in mind that similar faerie assistants are linked to each other. Thus dragons have a natural link, unicorns of various sorts are linked, rainbow dragons and rainbow serpents are linked and so on.

However, you may also wish to consider the elemental aspect of the spirit. Is this a water spirit, a fire spirit, an earth spirit, or an air spirit? Water spirits tend to get along together, but water and fire spirits are an uneasy association. Thus while dragons may be linked, two water dragons or water spirits will tend to associate more closely than a water and a fire dragon will. The stronger the number of links between your spirit and the spirit you may wish to evoke the closer the association and the easier the evocation.

You can, however, follow the lines of association. That is to say you evoke a spirit closely linked to your birth spirit and then follow that spirit's lines of association to another spirit and so on. This is like a friend introducing you to someone else, who introduces you to another person, and that person to another.

You may note that some of the Faerie Assistants are seen as being dangerous, malefic or harmful to mankind. These spirits, like you and all other life, are evolving and those who are assisting a particular Shining One are doing so because they have put aside their wickedness and are striving through this association to clear their karma and make their own evolutionary progress.

Also, note that some of these assistants are individual beings or an individual mythological or legendary figure. However, you should know that we are only using this figure as an example of a type of spirit and it does not, in fact, represent just one spirit. For instance, if we had Pan as a Faerie assistant, it would mean that all Pan figures, all satyrs would be indicated as assisting that Shining One.

Constellations

The names of the constellations are given in Arvyndase (see our book *Arvyndase (Silver Speech): a Short Course in the Magical Language of the Silver Elves*) and then their English name is given. If you wish to know more about the elven constellations or the magic/powers, such as the Cauldron of Rebirth, of each spirit you will find a deeper explanation in our book *The Elven Star Oracle*.

Continents

You will notice that the ruling spirits of each month are associated with a particular continent or area. This, of course, obviously doesn't mean you were born there but that there is a special magic for you in linking to that area. Certainly, you can evoke these spirits in traveling to, through, or dealing with anyone in that area. Also, the area where you were born, or are currently living, gives you an associative link to the ruling spirits there.

A Word About Pronouns

The English language does not have a pronoun that covers both male and female in instances when it could be either. For instance, if we wrote, "The magician did the magic and then left his or her magic circle", this would be correct English, but this "his or her", or "his/her", seems cumbersome to us. Most people write, "The magician did the magic and then left their magic circle." This creates incorrect correlation between singular and plural, but is common usage. We have instead settled upon the use of "hir" which combines his and her, and sHe or SHe that combines she and he as an alternative.

JANUARY

ÅNDIËL : TRANSFORMS DARKNESS

MONTH: JANUARY

MAGIC: THAUMATURGY

CONTINENT: AFRICA AND MADAGASGAR

CONSTELLATION: JOLOR, CYGNUS

PLANETARY ASSOCIATION: JUPITER

FAERIE ASSISTANTS: AZIZA

This Shining Ones rules the month of January and all born within it are under his guidance. He teaches the power of Thaumaturgy, that is the working of miracles and all who study this magical art come under his influence. He is also the over-guide for those born in Africa or Madagasgar or who currently live there, or whose ancestors come from there. He also preserves ancient scrolls, books and teachings of all sorts, particularly the Secret Doctrines of the world and thus is a guardian spirit of Librarians and metaphysical writers (see *Creating Miracles in the Modern World: The Way of the Elfin Thaumaturge*).

SOME FOLKS THINK WE ELVES DO NOTHING BUT LAUGH AND PLAY. OTHERS IMAGINE WE ARE SERIOUS PEOPLE WHO NEVER LAUGH. IN TRUTH, WE SEEK THE BALANCE IN ALL THINGS SEEKING TO ENJOY WHAT WE DO AND DOING WHAT WE ENJOY.

Shådandral: Sees the Miraculous
JANUARY 1ST THROUGH 10TH

MAGIC: THAURMAVOYANCE
AREA: WESTERN AFRICA
CONSTELLATION: JUFI, OCTANS
PLANETARY ASSOCIATION: MARS
FAERIE ASSISTANTS: SIMBI

This Shining Ones aides the elf to see the miraculous/magical nature of life, to see Faerie and our kind all around us. He is a very active spirit, being associated with Mars. This spirit also helps one understand the meaning behind the cycles of creation and destruction and how to ride the waves of the world without being overwhelmed by them. The elf under his influence comes to understand the bigger picture and sees hir (his/her) life in terms of the evolution of hir spirit through lifetimes and also to see the possibilities of miraculous power that awaits hir future.

Solynal: Everyday Miracles
JANUARY 11TH THROUGH 20TH

MAGIC: PRACTICAL MIRACLE WORKING
AREA: EASTERN AFRICA
CONSTELLATION: RYND, EQUULEUS
PLANETARY ASSOCIATION: NEPTUNE
FAERIE ASSISTANTS: YUMBOES

Solynal teaches the elven magician to create small or everyday miracles. She is associated with Neptune and thus evokes the power of the imagination and fantasy as a key to magical power. She helps one understand how magic can be inserted into everyday activities so that even vacuuming the floor can be a magical act. In this way, the elf gains magical power in all that sHe (he/she) does.

Sålåal: Inner Miracles
JANUARY 21ST THROUGH 31ST

MAGIC: THAURMA-INVOCATION
AREA: MADAGASGAR
CONSTELLATION: PAVOCA, PAVO
PLANETARY ASSOCIATION: URANUS
FAERIE ASSISTANTS: MAMI WATA

Sålåal helps the elf invoke the miraculous within hir, becoming in that way ever more magical as a being so hir mere presence radiates enchantment. He is assisted by the Mami Wata, who are great water spirits, and thus relationship and vibratory being is an important part of his teachings. He also aids the elfin in clearing hir karma and in purifying hir being so it is a fit receptacle for magic. As the magician becomes increasingly clear within, hir powers soar to ever-greater heights of magical manifestation increasingly becoming the Shining One sHe was always destined to be.

JANUARY 1ST
Nidyndre: One Who Creates Miracles

MAGIC: SACRED POOL
CONSTELLATION: MIHAN, ORION
PLANETARY ASSOCIATION: EARTH
FAERIE ASSISTANTS: NCONZO NKILA

This Shining One aids the elf in developing hir powers of Thaumaturgy, that is creating what seem to be miracles, by awakening to and utilizing the higher laws of the Universe that supersede the laws of the world, realm or dimension that elf finds hirs'elf within.

The elf who comes under the guidance of this spirit becomes increasingly aware of the extent of hir own power and the limitations sHe faces in the world, that is to say sHe knows what sHe can accomplish and what is beyond hir current power. Thus sHe is in the process of developing hir faith and hir soulful connection to the Shining Ones and hir spiritual family in Faerie and to rely, when things are beyond hir power, on their aid and beneficence. That being said, it should be noted that the elfin born here tend to be very lucky in their ability to accomplish things or are often graced by fortuitous circumstances that seem miraculous to others.

January 2nd

Syndarthys: Brings Meaning

MAGIC: CAULDRON OF REBIRTH
CONSTELLATION: LUTRA, PISCES
PLANETARY ASSOCIATION: MARS
FAERIE ASSISTANTS: WERE-HYENAS

This spirit aids the elfin who are under her care to develop the power of meaning. Purpose and meaning become very important to those she guides and they can often be seen to strive toward or express a need for leading a meaningful life.

Elves born under the influence of this Shining One are very imaginative beings and become adept at changing the world by changing their worldview, thus they tend to associate with Starhawk's via W.E. Bulter's via Dion Fortune's definition of Magic as "the art of changing one's consciousness at will" as a means of affecting the world. These elves can be restless and are willing to take risks to remove thems'elves from boring situations.

They may become depressed if they feel stuck in meaningless relationships, jobs or situations.

January 3rd

Mårelys: Mind Mirror

Magic: Horn of Calling
Constellation: Mefit, Cepheus
Planetary Association: Venus
Faerie Assistants: Satyroi Nesioi

Mårelys aids those in her care to develop the capacity to intuit the thoughts and ideas of others, as well as reflect their personalities if need be to merge into any group or social setting. This power in time leads to the development of psychic insight and the ability to read thoughts directly. These elves often find that they just know what others are thinking.

Those under her care often tend to be impulsive and will plunge into new projects with great enthusiasm. However, they need to develop a certain amount of prudence, for they can have a habit of burning thems'elves out after their initial efforts and thus give up, or find that they have plunged thems'elves into situations they don't really want to be in, or be prone to manic-depressive episodes. However, since they can change so easily they also tend to get thems'elves out of things as quickly and as easily as they plunged into them.

> *If you ask the elves what their favorite color is, they may very well tell you it is rainbow.*

JANUARY 4TH
Orynthel: Power of the Spirit
MAGIC: THE STONE OF THE LAND
CONSTELLATION: RAGOL, VIRGO
PLANETARY ASSOCIATION: EARTH
FAERIE ASSISTANTS: WERE-JACKALS

The elves under the guidance of Orynthel are developing the powers of enthusiasm and can be very exciting to be around. Their pure energy is attractive and their enthusiastic approach to life empowers others around them. Thus these elves can be very excitable and impulsive but particularly about starting new things. They are great s'elf starters or initiators and need to develop the capacity of endurance. They can be a bit naïve at times for just as their enthusiasm is appealing to others they get excited by things and people they encounter very easily thus they can tend to go from one fad to another. Their training under this Shining One is directed toward stabilizing their energy so they can retain their enthusiastic approach to life without exhausting thems'elves.

JANUARY 5TH
Verfarfyn: True to One's Soul
MAGIC: CAULDRON OF REBIRTH
CONSTELLATION: ECH, HERCULES
PLANETARY ASSOCIATION: SUN
FAERIE ASSISTANTS: WOKULO

This spirit helps those under his care to pay close attention to their instincts, particularly their sense of what is fair and just, and to ever seek the facts and the underlying truth in every situation. Because of this you can often find these elfin fighting to bring out justice in the world.

Due to this spirit's guidance these elfin tend to be mature and developed spirits often quite serious and purposeful and have a magnetic appeal to those of a similar nature. While they are passionate in their cause they are often cool and detached in their approach using reason and fact as a basis for their actions. They have come to understand the power of logic in the world and seek to reveal the truth where lies have held sway.

JANUARY 6TH

Zavorfyn: Wonder of Simple Things

MAGIC: SACRED POOL

CONSTELLATION: VANUS, VOLANS

PLANETARY ASSOCIATION: SATURN

FAERIE ASSISTANTS: DAN AYIDO HWEDO

Those under this spirit's care are taught to appreciate the simple things in life and in that sense are gaining the child-like point of view that sages nearly always demonstrate.

The individuals under Zavorfyn's guidance learn to live in the eye of the storm, the calm center in the midst of a world that seems to have gone mad. They are well aware of the many pressures and limitations placed upon them in the world but are coming to a place where these no longer affect them, which is to say they are less prone to stress than most folks and thus, as well, less prone to stress related diseases as they develop the capacity for calm appreciation of life's many gifts.

> WHILE MOST PEOPLE ARE BUSY TRYING TO MAKE IT IN THE WORLD, THE ELVES ARE BUSY CREATING IT.

JANUARY 7TH

Herofyn: Going Ever Onward

MAGIC: CAULDRON OF ABUNDANCE, CORNUCOPIA
CONSTELLATION: SARTH, VELA
PLANETARY ASSOCIATION: PLUTO
FAERIE ASSISTANTS: GEMSBOK

The elves who are influenced by Herofyn are learning to persevere despite all obstructions and obstacles. They learn to never give up and tend to be the very last ones to quit and will at times face death if necessary to achieve what they will.

These elves have a great store of inner experience, that is to say they are often called old souls, for their view of life includes their understanding of the wide range of evolution and their own instinctual awareness of the many lifetimes they have lived. They are well aware and very comfortable with the occult side of life and learn to see into the hidden side of all things, thus these tend to advance as magicians and occultists very quickly though this life as their early life is a recapitulation of profound progress in earlier lifetimes.

JANUARY 8TH

Arånåfyl: Among the Mountains

MAGIC: THE STONE OF THE LAND
CONSTELLATION: ARANDUS, RETICULUM
PLANETARY ASSOCIATION: URANUS
FAERIE ASSISTANTS: MALXAS

This is the spirit that can move mountains. Those under her care often start out in life as very conservative and staid individuals only to become more and more liberal in their views as they progress.

Because of this they tend to seem young even when they grow old, they are the people that are spoken of as being young at heart, or who say you are only as old as you think, act or feel. Thus the older they get, the more flighty they seem for they are in the process of freeing their emotional s'elves, easing up their grip upon their reactions, and learning to be spontaneous.

JANUARY 9TH

Oryndel: Ponders the Wondrous

MAGIC: FAERY CIRCLE
CONSTELLATION: GRADLI, TUCANA
PLANETARY ASSOCIATION: VENUS
FAERIE ASSISTANTS: OSHUMAIRE

Oryndel aids those in her care to gain energy from association. Thus these elfin are energized greatly from gatherings and often serve to help organize them. They are very relationship oriented and are in the process of learning the power that comes from soulful connections. At the same time, Oryndel aids the elf under her guidance to hold hir own in a group, that is to say maintain or develop hir own thoughts and point of view even while associating with others. These elves are increasingly learning to overcome peer pressure and enculturation.

The elves born under this spirit tend to be optimistic by nature and develop a great vision of the future and the possibilities of what the future will bring; they often strive to create utopian societies.

IT IS SAID THAT MOST WOMEN LOVE A MAN IN UNIFORM. ELVES LOVE AN ELF IN COSTUME.

January 10th

Vorlasyn: Unseen Mind

Magic: Spear of Light and Destiny
Constellation: Janel, Grus
Planetary Association: Asteroids
Faerie Assistants: Diff Errebi

This Shining One arouses purpose in those under his influence and inspires them with Quests to fulfill and things to be accomplished as well as a sense of their own power to do these things. The longer one is under this spirit's aegis the more powerful one feels.

These individuals often function as lawyers or in the legal system, either mundane or cosmic, and learn how to operate within and use the system in order to achieve justice. They usually become deeply committed to affecting changes through or within the system rather than outside of it.

January 11th

Gradarfyn: Friend of the Forest

Magic: Horn of Calling
Constellation: Atarold, Monoceros
Planetary Association: Moon
Faerie Assistants: Bida

This spirit inspires a love of Nature in those he guides but also bestows the power to gather others. Elves under this spirit's guidance are often stewards of Nature sanctuaries or protectors of the forest or wild places.

Those born here can be very intuitive, even clairvoyant, or are developing those skills but can also be emotionally vulnerable and excitable. It is these that one often finds struggling with their psychic skills, uncertain as yet whether their abilities are a gift or a curse or both. They often feel overwhelmed by the influx of psychic impressions and spend this life learning to control this power so they don't feel under constant or periodic assault by the emotions and thoughts of others, which in part may be what attracts them about wild places where they can get away from the mass of humanity and its emotional turmoil.

January 12th
Dilethyn: Compassion's Choice
Magic: Horn of Calling
Constellation: Vanus, Volans
Planetary Association: Asteroids
Faerie Assistants: Were-Leopards

Dilethyn teaches the healing arts, particularly psychological healing, thus those under her care often pursue careers as therapists in one form or another. Their compassionate understanding makes others feel they are trustworthy individuals and thus people often reveal their secrets to the elves influenced by this Shining One.

Alas, because of their deep empathy and sympathy for those under their care they tend to form personal, even sexual, relationships with them that may violate the ethical code of their profession. Also, those under the care of these fae tend often to fall in love with them, which is where the temptation begins. Part of what they are doing in this life is learning to resist the temptation to become involved with those who are, as yet, not on their level of spiritual and emotional development. They need to accept the fact and responsibility of being an advanced adept.

> THE SHINING ONES SAY WE ARE DROPLETS OF FIRE IN AN OCEAN OF LIGHT.

The Silver Elves

January 13th
Farynfar: Evokes Miracles

MAGIC: THE MAGIC MIRROR
CONSTELLATION: PIHYR, SEXTANS
PLANETARY ASSOCIATION: NEPTUNE
FAERIE ASSISTANTS: THAMUATZ

Those born under Farynfar's influence draw luck and the lucky to thems'elves. They are deeply affected by those around them, so being in the right company is extremely important for their progress. They need to avoid bad or unworthy companionship at all costs.

These elves tend to come into life accepting whatever they have been told and it is often a great shock to them when they learn that the world, their parents, family, government, country, ethnic group, or religion is not all that it has claimed to be. It is at this point that they are compelled to seek the higher way by finding advanced adepts and learning from them. In many instances, they become translators or ambassadors, so to speak, who make the influence of the Shining Ones understandable to those less adept than they.

January 14th
Norelyn: Only This Once

MAGIC: SACRED POOL
CONSTELLATION: RIFRO, PHOENIX
PLANETARY ASSOCIATION: JUPITER
FAERIE ASSISTANTS: UNWARA

The elfin who come under this spirit's purview are often willing to try anything once and thus need to be very cautious of those things that are quickly addictive. Needless to say they can be somewhat daring, if heedless, individuals.

These fae can be transformative beings, they accept new ideas easily and learn to express thems'elves with great ability thus they make great teachers and if we elves were into proselytizing, which we are not, they would be fantastic preachers. They are often the source of enlightenment to others and tend to stir up the world wherever they go. People often feel revitalized or reborn after meeting them.

JANUARY 15TH

Jåndila: Homeward Bound

MAGIC: THE STONE OF THE LAND
CONSTELLATION: URMA, DORADO
PLANETARY ASSOCIATION: EARTH
FAERIE ASSISTANTS: SIGI

Jåndila is the patron of those who create Elven Homes, or sanctuaries for our kind. She encourages elves to create communities, vortexes and other groups so they may function together in the world.

These fae learn to express what they feel clearly without consideration of what is socially acceptable. Harmonious and peaceful environments are important to them but they are unwilling to repress their feelings to gain social acceptance. If they find thems'elves in a stressful situation they will either get sick or leave if their pleas for harmony go unheeded. Naturally, they seek to be with those who are easily compatible to them; they do not thrive well in argumentative relationships nor do they wish to be in homes where people are constantly arguing or fighting. Rather they seek to be where people can talk freely about their ideas and feelings without conflict or judgments.

January 16th

Lenafyn: Looks For the Source

MAGIC: HORN OF CALLING

CONSTELLATION: RYSTATA, CAELUM

PLANETARY ASSOCIATION: JUPITER

FAERIE ASSISTANTS: OSTRICH

This spirit inspires those in her care to seek the roots of all things. Therefore, those under her guidance often have an interest in history, how things work, how they were invented and are ever endeavoring to understand why things are the way they are, and how they got to be that way.

They are often very sympathetic individuals who have been through a lot in their immediate or previously lifetimes, and thus easily understand the struggles of others. They often seem mature beyond their years, even when very young, and frequently exude an air of dignity and forbearance; they thus tend to develop into very good mentors and parents.

January 17th

Wyladyn: Yearns to Return Home

MAGIC: FAERY CIRCLE

CONSTELLATION: LOWA, ERIDANUS

PLANETARY ASSOCIATION: MERCURY

FAERIE ASSISTANTS: ELAND

These individuals, under the care of Wyladyn, never forget their past, their home or their upbringing and even if reared in a dysfunctional fashion seek to recreate their home life in a more positive and fulfilling way.

It is very important that these individuals find the right mates, for to fail to do so can result in years of misery, as they are determined to make their family life work and will thus put up with agonizing situations for a long time in an effort to make things work out. They are loyal and faithful friends who will carry those they have loved in their hearts long after they have departed. They do not always need a lot of people about them but they very much long for at least one true and faithful friend/lover.

JANUARY 18TH

Hylynle: Growing More Beautiful With Age

MAGIC: FAERY CIRCLE
CONSTELLATION: FOLI, LYRA
PLANETARY ASSOCIATION: JUPITER
FAERIE ASSISTANTS: SORE-GUS

These individuals under Hylynle's supervision, like her, grow more beautiful with age and in extension often have a love of antiques and other things, such as certain wines, whose quality, beauty or value increases as it ages. At the same time, Hylynle teaches these elves how to see beauty where others do not and they can often become Divvies who have an instinctual feel for what are true antiques or things of value or things that will become valuable in time. (see the TV series or books about *Lovejoy*).

The elves born in this place are often disciplined, energetic and ambitious. They have an instinctual understanding of business and usually are quite successful financially even when pursuing non-traditional careers.

FOR THE FAERIES, GLITTER IS NOT JUST AN ART SUPPLY, IT'S A WAY OF LIFE.

The Silver Elves

JANUARY 19ᵀᴴ
Zyndåle: Yearns for Completion
MAGIC: CAULDRON OF ABUNDANCE, CORNUCOPIA
CONSTELLATION: SETÅTRU, OPHIUCUS
PLANETARY ASSOCIATION: ASTEROIDS
FAERIE ASSISTANTS: PEGASI AITHIOPES

Zyndåle inspires the fae in her care to bring things to completion. Those who learn from her often become "closers" able to seal the deal in due time. Sometimes they are a variety of reapers, when they arrive it is usually just after a situation has peaked and is on the downhill slide.

These individuals usually signify the end. They come to finish things up and the world around them is seldom the same after they leave. Often these elfin arrive en masse when one root race is giving way to another, or one sub-race to another, which is to say at the end of an era or aeon. They tend to close things down, and in their youth are often described as *bringing the house down*. They also make good counselors for the dying.

JANUARY 20ᵀᴴ
Nenareyn: Offers the Help of the Fae
MAGIC: SPEAR OF LIGHT AND DESTINY
CONSTELLATION: PYKTAR, SAGITTA
PLANETARY ASSOCIATION: EARTH
FAERIE ASSISTANTS: WUTE

The elves influenced by Nenareyn feel they have a destiny to fulfill and know that the Shining Ones have sent them to achieve something important. You might think they would therefore be tense individuals but in actuality they become quite confident and certain of what they are doing and very relaxed in their approach to life, as only the powerful and experienced tend to be. There is little that fazes them and they are always ready to spring into action if need be.

JANUARY 21ST

Gilynre: For the Foreseeable Future

MAGIC: FAERY CIRCLE
CONSTELLATION: PIHYR, SEXTANS
PLANETARY ASSOCIATION: VENUS
FAERIE ASSISTANTS: KIVUNGA

Those born under this spirit have taken a vow to manifest Faerie on Earth and they are quite serious in their dedication to doing so. Quite often they have failed at this previously and vowed that in this lifetime they will not fail or abandon their cause. They tend to be group-oriented individuals and are keen to organize and get things going. Their capacity for accomplishing this task increases as they study under Gilynre.

These elves tend to be attractive, sensitive to the feelings of others and have the ability to understand others easily. They often awaken love or attraction in others with no conscious effort on their part, which is, of course, quite helpful in their Quest.

WHEN WE ELVES ARE TOLD TO STOP DOING SOMETHING THAT WE HAVEN'T DONE, WE OFTEN INTERPRET THAT TO MEAN WE SHOULD START.

January 22nd

Udidyn: Teaches the Way

Magic: Cauldron of Abundance, Cornucopia
Constellation: Pavoca, Pavo
Planetary Association: Pluto
Faerie Assistants: Itherther

Udidyn often guides teachers. She teaches how to teach and how to be generous in helping and nurturing others. She is particularly nurturing of eccentrics who are often the prototypes for new species and sub-species of being.

These elves often like to have a lot of friends and lovers, and to play the field, so to speak, and thus sometimes come into conflict with traditional societies and relationships where free love is seen as cheating. They are often experimenters of new types of social interaction. They don't always succeed in these new forms, but they are, after all, only experimenting.

January 23rd

Tyleåvyn: How I See Mys'elf

Magic: The Rings of Power
Constellation: Acantha, Circinus
Planetary Association: Moon
Faerie Assistants: Goli

This spirit aids those under his care to develop s'elf confidence and increasingly understand their personal power. Ceremonial Magick is often attractive to these elfin.

These fae develop s'elf control, are often prone to be the ones who go on meditation retreats or withdraw into caves to contemplate, or go into the wild for a vision quest. They develop great emotional strength and thus are seen as being very stable or a stabilizing influence. At the same time, because of their frequently meditative and contemplative nature they are often perceived as mysterious and as having secret powers or knowledge that ordinary folk do not possess.

JANUARY 24TH

Imordre: Healing Thoughts

MAGIC: SHIELD OF LOVE AND PROTECTION
CONSTELLATION: JANEL, GRUS
PLANETARY ASSOCIATION: EARTH
FAERIE ASSISTANTS: BUMBA

Imordre, as her name suggests, is a very healing spirit and protects those in her care. Naturally, the elves she guides are her apprentices and are often protective and or healing individuals thems'elves.

These fae are very intelligent and independent thinkers, are quick to say what they think as well as quick to change what they think if a better idea occurs to them. They delight in clever conversation and dialogue and even when they don't know about a particular subject often bring new and fresh ways of viewing it, much like a child would. In this way, they are often like Dr. Watson to Sherlock Holmes who while unable to solve the crime himself was often the inspiration for Sherlock's solution without realizing it.

> *THE ELVES ARE A BIT LIKE COMETS TRAVELING THROUGH THE REALMS AND SHEDDING LIGHT WHEREVER THEY GO.*

January 25th

Thordyndor: Started to See

MAGIC: HORN OF CALLING

CONSTELLATION: SARTH, VELA

PLANETARY ASSOCIATION: SATURN

FAERIE ASSISTANTS: YUMBOES

The elfin under this spirit's aegis generally are just opening their eyes and understanding to new levels of awareness. This is true whether they are novices or advanced adepts who have moved to a new and greater initiation.

These individuals are often well aware of their unique status of being new to something and yet bearing the potential for greatness in that area. They are often seen as prodigies. Sometimes they have deliberately started anew, like a painter or musician who has tired of hir previous style and seeks to test hirs'elf in a new media or genre. But even at the beginning of things these tend to plunge in directly and with passionate fervor, confident in their ultimate mastery of anything they undertake.

January 26th

Zuryndra: Yearning to Set Them Free

MAGIC: CAULDRON OF REBIRTH

CONSTELLATION: ULOS, TAURUS

PLANETARY ASSOCIATION: MOON

FAERIE ASSISTANTS: CALLITRICE

The elfin born under this spirit have often returned to Earth to awaken others of our kind and to help make a better world. It is quite possible that they have chosen to be here and are not held to this world by karma but by love, dedication and a desire to help.

These are often Earth Mother types, whether they are male or female, and create loving, nurturing environments for fae to heal, grow and prosper within. Every elven vortex is better off having one of this type within it. With the aid of these elfin the transition to one's elven nature is easier and one quickly gives up the enculturated doubts that had bound one to the world. These fae are especially a comfort to those who are distressed or in need, and they seem to have a mystical ability to soothe and heal.

January 27th

Såtarys: Shimmering Faerie Wings

MAGIC: SWORD OF TRUTH AND JUSTICE
CONSTELLATION: FOLI, LYRA
PLANETARY ASSOCIATION: MARS
FAERIE ASSISTANTS: CHIWARA

Those who come under this Shining One's influence are generally very active, energetic and action oriented. This spirit teaches those under his care to take decisive action for what is right and they are not inclined, generally, to put up with a lot of "guff" or "bullshit".

Sometimes, those born here struggle to accept thems'elves as they truly are, their natural s'elves having been rejected by normal society, so there is a need for concerted action to clarify within thems'elves what is true and not true. Because of this, these individuals sometimes go astray reacting to the world and wishing to strike back at it instead of plunging assuredly ahead; but in the course of evolution this is cleared up and when they are finally committed inexorably to their path they are transferred to the influence of other spirits. These elves especially need to be open to the guidance of signs and omens.

January 28th

Uforea: Tends Upward
MAGIC: SHIELD OF LOVE AND PROTECTION
CONSTELLATION: RALTOSOR, CORONA AUSTRALIS
PLANETARY ASSOCIATION: MOON
FAERIE ASSISTANTS: IMPUNDULU

The fae receiving the advice of this spirit are preparing to move much more deeply into Faerie, to leave this dimension for one of the more Elven dimensions that are parallel to it.

They are increasing their sensitivity as individuals, their receptivity and their ability to accurately pick up and/or channel the influence of the Faerie realms. Vibrationally, they become the living embodiment of Faerie, radiating its power into this realm. Because of their place between the worlds they often find thems'elves subject to feelings that they can't quite explain and frequently are unwilling to talk about. In fact, they are being readied for that *other* world and what is unfamiliar here will become quite common there. Because of this attunement to the Faerie realms they are naturally vulnerable as individuals and must take care to be in harmonious environments with those they can trust as much as possible, otherwise they tend to turn to drugs or alcohol to dull the pain of living in the mundane world.

SOME FOLKS TELL US THAT THE END IS RIGHT AROUND THE CORNER— WHICH IS WHY WE ELVES LIKE TO LIVE IN FORESTS WHERE THERE ARE NO CORNERS.

January 29th

Omåle: Path of Least Resistance

MAGIC: CAULDRON OF ABUNDANCE, CORNUCOPIA
CONSTELLATION: RAGOL, VIRGO
PLANETARY ASSOCIATION: VENUS
FAERIE ASSISTANTS: NDZOODZOO

Those who come under Omåle's influence become very efficient beings, able to accomplish a great deal with very little, who nearly always profit in every situation; a fact that develops an easy generosity within them. They know or learn that whatever they give will be returned to them manifold.

These elves are learning how to go through life without resisting it. The more they progress, the easier things become for them until they see every obstacle in their lives as a mere, and temporary, inconvenience. They often develop a serene inner nature that is unperturbed by stressful situations or people around them. They do need to be cautious of becoming cold and indifferent to the plight of others but they are very keen in realizing that people's reactions to problems often make the situation worse rather than better.

January 30th

Shirevyn: Singing to the Stars

MAGIC: THE RINGS OF POWER
CONSTELLATION: GATH, CRUX
PLANETARY ASSOCIATION: MERCURY
FAERIE ASSISTANTS: COWS OF NAKKI

Shirevyn is a star enchanter and shows those in her care how to summon up the power of the stars and direct it toward fulfilling their will. Thus those under her influence can have a profound grasp over the material world and develop in the course of their training the ability to get nearly anything they desire of a material nature. These elves must be careful of being drawn back into the values of normal society or to allow their material success to be the sole basis of their feelings of value and s'elf worth. They are called in this life to reach beyond mere material success, to see thems'elves as evolving beings, and to fully expand their spiritual and soulful natures.

January 31ST
Naeltyn: New Direction
MAGIC: CAULDRON OF ABUNDANCE, CORNUCOPIA
CONSTELLATION: ARELO, AURIGA
PLANETARY ASSOCIATION:
FAERIE ASSISTANTS: ADAMASTOR

Those who receive this spirit's help have often been unsuccessful or poor in previous lifetimes but are now ready to begin anew and to acquire skills that will increasingly bring them success. This new situation often creates a sense of boldness in them. They feel free or unburdened at last, have an intuitive sense of a certain weight of karma having been or being lifted from them and become increasingly confident as they mature. Like many who are new at something, they are often hesitant at first but become more and more daring in their approach as they explore and test the limits of their new abilities. Martin Luther King, Jr.'s words, '"Free at last, free at last, Thank God almighty we are free at last," often expresses the feelings of these elfin.

FEBRUARY

SUVARÈL: OPENS THE THRESHOLD

MONTH: FEBRUARY

MAGIC: ENCHANTMENT

CONTINENT: ARABIAN PENINSULA AND NORTHERN AFRICA

CONSTELLATION: KONALYMLE, HOROLOGIUM

PLANETARY ASSOCIATION: SUN

FAERIE ASSISTANTS: DJINN

Suvarèl guides all who are born in February, as well as having great influence during that month. She watches over those who are born or live in the Arabian Peninsula and Northern Africa. Also Persia, Pakistan and Afghanistan. She is assisted by the Djinn or genie of the deserts. She teaches enchantment to all interested in that magical art. She is also a protector of the innocent and can be evoked by those seeking to overcome addiction or master temptation or who are confronted by dark sorceries.

THE SHINING ONES GUIDE ALL WHO CALL TO THEM AND MANY WHO KNOW NOT OF THEIR EXISTENCE BUT ARE OF GOOD HEART AND STRIVING SPIRIT.

Zyndåal: Charms the Spirits
FEBRUARY 1ST TO 10TH

MAGIC: CHARMS, AMULETS AND TALISMANS
AREA: ARABIAN PENINSULA
CONSTELLATION: WAND (PRONOUNCED WANED), MICROSCOPIUM
PLANETARY ASSOCIATION: NEPTUNE
FAERIE ASSISTANTS: MARID

Zyndåal guides those born from the 1st to 10th of February and is particularly adept in the making of charms, amulets and talismans. He is assisted by the Marids who are a form of Djinn (read Jonathan Stroud's Bartimaeus novels). Any elf wishing to learn about the power of amulets, charms (such as charm bracelets), and talismans can evoke this spirit for assistance and those born under his influence would be naturally adept at this if they have any interest in this art, although his influence does not guarantee that interest. Also, any elf who might wish to evoke a Marid could get assistance from Zyndåal in doing so, or in introducing ones'elf first to Zyndåal get a recommendation. Zyndåal also can demonstrate the incredible power to create and promote growth in regions that otherwise seem entirely barren. Thus those who think of terraforming Mars or Martian-like places on Earth may seek his advice.

> *THE SHINING ONES ARE NOT GODS, ALTHOUGH SOME MAY THINK THEM SO FOR THEY ARE GREAT AND POWERFUL.*

Duryndal: Wondrously Bewitching
FEBRUARY 11TH TO 20TH

MAGIC: BEWITCHING
AREA: NORTHERN AFRICA
CONSTELLATION: RALTOSOR, CORONA AUSTRALIS
PLANETARY ASSOCIATION: MERCURY
FAERIE ASSISTANTS: AL RAKIM

Duryndal, assisted by the Al Rakim who are guard dogs and are thus associated with all guards and guard dog forms around the world. They are said to protect the Sleeping Seven and are therefore associated with the seven-pointed elven star and all sacred groupings of that magical number. Duryndal teaches the power of Bewitching and is a patron of all entertainers of every sort, from musicians to comedians to actors, and can be of great assistance to Enchanters. Duryndal also can teach of the magic of scents, particularly incense as well as the magic of chimes, gongs, bells, etc.

Paldåral: Reveals the Mysteries
FEBRUARY 21ST TO 29TH

MAGIC: EVOCATION OF MYSTERIES
AREA: PERSIA, AFGHANISTAN, PAKISTAN
CONSTELLATION: SETÅTRU, OPHIUCUS
PLANETARY ASSOCIATION: PLUTO
FAERIE ASSISTANTS: HOURI

The Shining One Paldåral is an initiator into the esoteric mysteries and is assisted by the Houri who are enchantresses and enchanters of higher levels and thus are thems'elves Shining Ones. Paldåral can teach one about the oils of anointing and how to create them in such a way as to awaken the inner spirit. This Shining One is also associated with healing, but particularly the healing of the psyche. She will further reveal the secrets of using aromas to evoke or instill memories.

FEBRUARY 1ST

Eriåfyn: Drifts Toward Beauty
MAGIC: SACRED POOL
CONSTELLATION: MATH, PYXIS
PLANETARY ASSOCIATION: MERCURY
FAERIE ASSISTANTS: AIGIPANES LIBYES

Eriåfyn guides those in her care to learn to increasingly appreciate beauty and its Divine and sacred underpinnings. Those under her training can become art historians, art gallery owners or others for whom art and its appreciation is a lifelong endeavor.

These individuals often have very active imaginations and convey their enthusiasms easily. With hard work and consistent effort they can obtain fame and fortune in their chosen careers. They frequently serve as the example that others in their fields emulate and they set the tone of their time and environment.

FEBRUARY 2ND

Neåvålyn: Of the Mist
MAGIC: THE MAGIC MIRROR
CONSTELLATION: ÅNLEA, ANTLIA
PLANETARY ASSOCIATION: URANUS
FAERIE ASSISTANTS: OG

This spirit develops the mystical qualities in those who were born under his care and their lives are often a reflection of the deeper worlds that are unseen to most folks thus they are frequently thought of as oracles with insight into the future or an ability to see into the invisible dimensions about us.

Because they tend to reflect the otherworldly, these elves often seem hard to pin down, as amorphous as the worlds they reflect. They can be very moody and changeable since their feelings and personalities are deeply affected by the atmosphere of the netherworlds. Those who meet these individuals often say that they are "off with the faeries".

FEBRUARY 3RD

Borynfa: Beneath the Surface

MAGIC: SHIELD OF LOVE AND PROTECTION
CONSTELLATION: MIHAN, ORION
PLANETARY ASSOCIATION: ASTEROIDS
FAERIE ASSISTANTS: BAHAMUT

The elves who are being trained by this spirit learn to be gentle and yielding on the surface while being rock hard within. Thus those who think they are easy prey are greatly mistaken and come to regret their error.

Because of their tremendous inner strength these elves come to be greatly admired and as they mature become powerful and magnetic personalities. They usually obtain what they want in the world and can be counted on by those with whom they associate. Their word is their bond and you can trust that when they make a promise they will keep it.

> THE SHINING ONES ARE MARINERS IN AN OCEAN OF STARLIGHT.

FEBRUARY 4ᵀᴴ

Gåndorfyn: Flew Near

MAGIC: SWORD OF TRUTH AND JUSTICE
CONSTELLATION: LARCA, LEO
PLANETARY ASSOCIATION: PLUTO
FAERIE ASSISTANTS: QARIN

This spirit helps elves define what is true about thems'elves, what is a reflection of their true natures and what is extraneous stuff placed in their psyches by others. He aids them to polish and refine their personalities and they learn to become ever more efficient in their actions. They are often said to be "comfortable in their own bodies".

These elves also come to understand what is true and not true of the Faerie worlds. They sort legend and folklore from reality and clarify the way for others to come. Although, Faerie is a changing and protean reality, these elves help one to find the first secure steps into that fantastic world.

FEBRUARY 5ᵀᴴ

Zyryndyn: Young Enchanter

MAGIC: STAFF OF POWER
CONSTELLATION: HOLVORO, FORNAX
PLANETARY ASSOCIATION: JUPITER
FAERIE ASSISTANTS: MERMEN

The elves in this spirit's care are just learning the powers of enchantment and developing their own abilities therein. They are often unusual or distinctive in appearance, not fitting the social norm for beauty yet having a mysterious aura that attracts others to their unique nature. There is just something different about them.

The Shining Ones

These individuals enjoy the sensual aspects of life and attract abundance. They often obtain easy popularity for they are not only attractive in a mysterious way but also obliging to others for they have known rejection in previous lifetimes and have developed great sympathy for the unusual and the eccentric. They do need to be cautious of overindulgence since plenty comes easily to them and discipline is something they are still developing.

FEBRUARY 6TH

Tulorvyn: Survived Great Danger

MAGIC: SACRED POOL
CONSTELLATION: LANU, ARA
PLANETARY ASSOCIATION: VENUS
FAERIE ASSISTANTS: IFRITS

Those under this spirit's influence have a sense of being survivors even when the great dangers and tragedies they survived were in previous lifetimes. Because of what they have been through they can be deeply empathetic and sympathetic individuals.

They none-the-less are still frequently filled with a sense that everything could fall apart at any moment and are learning to see and trust in the higher movements and progress of evolution and to have faith in the Shining Ones and the cosmic forces that move the Universe. In time, this leads to a deep inner stability that is unperturbed by anything that may happen in the outer world.

> *SOME PEOPLE THINK THE APOCALYPSE IS INEVITABLE. WE ELVES THINK IT IS THE INEVITABLE CONSEQUENCE OF OBSTINENT STUPIDITY.*

February 7th
Pålådredyn: Preparing for the Future
MAGIC: FAERY CIRCLE
CONSTELLATION: FADON LUPRAE, CANIS MAJOR
PLANETARY ASSOCIATION: MERCURY
FAERIE ASSISTANTS: MARIDS

Pålådredyn's apprentices are taught to have an eye on the future and ever look to the way things can be rather than feeling bound by the way things are. They always see possibility.

These fae become very nurturing individuals, have a strong sense of family and are continually seeking to create an elven family in their lives. Their giving natures empower those around them and often they take others under their wing who are like them and train them in the arts of family creation as well. They work very well with others and often run things behind the scenes with few even realizing the guidance they are getting.

February 8th
Ularvyn: That Is Truly Magic
MAGIC: FAERY CIRCLE
CONSTELLATION: ACANTHA, CIRCINUS
PLANETARY ASSOCIATION: JUPITER
FAERIE ASSISTANTS: KARKADANN

Those in Ularvyn's school of evolutionary education learn how to make the magic real, that is create an magical atmosphere so that others of a sensitive nature or with the Sight and with enough occult maturity can easily perceive the magic around them. Even those who are less sensitive often feel that something amazing is going on even if they can't quite put their finger on what it is.

These elves become very persuasive individuals who are good at promoting whatever cause they deem worthy. They tend to be compassionate and generous, particularly of their time and their understanding. They are eager to help others to comprehend what they are telling them and thus they make good teachers.

FEBRUARY 9TH

Urvynfe: There Is More to it than it Seems

MAGIC: THE MAGIC MIRROR
CONSTELLATION: SALMO, PISCES AUSTRINUS
PLANETARY ASSOCIATION: SATURN
FAERIE ASSISTANTS: GRINE

Urvynfe shows those under her influence that there is more to the world than can be seen and this frequently leads them to careers or a deep interest in the occult, micro-biology or quantum physics. She also reveals how the principle of As Above/So Below functions in practical terms in the world.

Alas, this greater understanding of the Universe makes them seem like lunatics to those for whom the world is a square and reality solid. They can tend to shake up people's worldviews and many hide in confusion or grasp at ignorance in order to save themselves from having to actually think about the mysterious nature of reality. Thus these elves tend to find friends among those who share their understanding, or they learn to keep their deeper insights to thems'elves lest they be thought insane by normal folk.

> *WE ELVES SOMETIMES CALL THE APOCALYPSE THE "END OF AN ERROR".*

FEBRUARY 10TH
Wyledyn: Watches the Changes
MAGIC: FAERY CIRCLE
CONSTELLATION: ÅNLEA, ANTLIA
PLANETARY ASSOCIATION: NEPTUNE
FAERIE ASSISTANTS: ANZU

Wyledyn is a Watcher, an observer, and teaches those under her care to do the same, that is to watch with keen perception and understanding. These elves may be said to take the pulse of the world from time to time.

It is not that these elves never act, but that they ever keep a check on what is going on and report that to those who need to know. Among normal folk they would probably be the community watch, among elves they monitor the ambience of the vortex seeing what is or will be needed and act to secure things before they are required or things get out of balance. These elves make sure the supply is always adequate.

FEBRUARY 11TH
Redynve: Secret Keeper
MAGIC: HORN OF CALLING
CONSTELLATION: ROCHILA, PEGASUS
PLANETARY ASSOCIATION: MOON
FAERIE ASSISTANTS: SIRIS

Redynve summons advancing adepts to higher development and understanding. Those born under her influence are slotted to advance in this life from whatever position they currently hold.

The elves born here often get a springtime like feeling about their life, or feel they are being reborn in this life, for they sense they are about to enter or have just entered a whole new world of perceptual experience. Thus they often fall in love with others they meet on this path although these bonds are sometimes temporary rather than permanent as first love frequently is. As they advance these elves learn secrets that are only available to those of their advanced status.

February 12th

Wylyndyn: Watches the World Go Round

Magic: Staff of Power
Constellation: Janel, Grus
Planetary Association: Uranus
Faerie Assistants: Ninurta

This spirit teaches the elfin in her care about how to see, understand and utilize the cycles of Nature and the Universe. This is a deep and profound magic that enables those who truly understand it to accomplish profound things.

These elves are very creative and are not the type to begin things and abandon them quickly. They see things to completion and delight in the product of their creativity, thus their homes are often filled with the art or crafts they have created or awards or other indicators of the things they have achieved. This is not hubris on their part but a true pleasure and delight in the results of their efforts. Naturally, they love to be praised for their creativity but are also learning how to appreciate the creativity of others.

> WE ELVES SRIVE TO MAKE OURSELVES AT HOME EVERYWHERE.

FEBRUARY 13TH

Onere: People Person
MAGIC: FAERY CIRCLE
CONSTELLATION: ARAK, SAGITTARIUS
PLANETARY ASSOCIATION: NEPTUNE
FAERIE ASSISTANTS: LORD SAMAN-ANA

This Shining One teaches those born under her influence how to "make friends and influence people". These fae are either those who are good at organizing gatherings or are learning how to do so. If you hate being around people and are a committed introvert you may wish to ask yours'elf why the Shining Ones put you under this spirit's care and what you need to learn from her to move on.

The elves who progress under this spirit attain great leadership ability and become very confident in their capacity to deal with others and guide them effectively. Many of these elves are being primed to be Shining Ones who will soon guide others in future lifetimes.

FEBRUARY 14TH

Gylelys: Fun to be Around
MAGIC: SACRED POOL
CONSTELLATION: FAERO, TRIANGULUM
PLANETARY ASSOCIATION: SATURN
FAERIE ASSISTANTS: CHAMROSH

Gylelys helps those in her care to become a source of fun and joy for others. They come to be admired and help people feel better and more optimistic about life.

Strangely, this lightness of spirit that these elfin exude often releases a well of emotion in the others that are around them.

The Shining Ones

People are touched very deeply by these fae although at first they don't always realize it. Somehow these elves remind others of when they were young and innocent and the world seemed more magical and everything wondrous was possible, of forgotten dreams and future possibilities.

FEBRUARY 15™

Wivevyn: Wants It All

MAGIC: STAFF OF POWER
CONSTELLATION: DRAKAN, DRACO
PLANETARY ASSOCIATION: NEPTUNE
FAERIE ASSISTANTS: AŽIS

This Shining One encourages those in his care to go for it, to achieve all they can, to pursue their dreams fully and with passion, revealing to them that no effort is ever lost, even if they fail in a particular task, and all serves to make them stronger and more powerful.

Realizing that much of what they wish to achieve cannot be done alone these individuals increasingly develop the ability to organize others toward a common goal as well as develop the ability to persuade them of the worthiness and value of that goal. At the same time, these elves become very practical individuals who see what really needs to be done to make something work and not mere fantasists as some who hear them may think.

> *IF SOMEONE TELLS THE ELVES TO MAKE OURSELVES AT HOME, WE DO AND START LOOKING FOR CLOSET SPACE AND DISHES TO DO.*

The Silver Elves

FEBRUARY 16TH
Umarfyn: That's the Way of It
MAGIC: THE STONE OF THE LAND
CONSTELLATION: WAND, MICROSCOPIUM
PLANETARY ASSOCIATION: PLUTO
FAERIE ASSISTANTS: PERI

This spirit helps those under her care to increasingly learn practicality and acceptance of their current position and status in the hierarchy of evolutionary development so that they can make rapid progress instead of struggling with their fate.

In coming to accept her guidance, these elves find that the effort they make in this life will truly open opportunities in the future and that their struggles in life are not in vain. As they mature, these elfin become increasingly stable and reliable as individuals, so much so that sometimes they are referred to as being like a rock.

FEBRUARY 17TH
Dråkynde: Crystal Clear Vision
MAGIC: SHIELD OF LOVE AND PROTECTION
CONSTELLATION: TARUNTUS, HYDRUS
PLANETARY ASSOCIATION: EARTH
FAERIE ASSISTANTS: MALEK KHAZEN

The elfin under this spirit's care obtain the ability to see into people's hearts and know what these folks are truly feeling or experiencing; thus they easily communicate with others and find thems'elves welcomed nearly anywhere they go. These fae, in consequence, often have a love of traveling, especially to new and different places and are usually quick to learn other languages, easily fitting in with the people and culture. Therefore any profession that allows them to travel fits well with their disposition.

The highest adepts of this type will, of course, be learning to travel from one parallel world to another.

FEBRUARY 18ᵀᴴ
Raådyn: Rowan Branch
MAGIC: STAFF OF POWER
CONSTELLATION: PRASUGAE, LUPUS
PLANETARY ASSOCIATION: VENUS
FAERIE ASSISTANTS: ROC

Raådyn helps those under his influence learn the principles of psychic s'elf defense and the power to move safely through the various astral planes.

These elves develop the ability to effortlessly communicate their intentions upon the subtle planes of manifestation and thus are in the process of becoming powerful magicians, sorcerers, wizards, etc. They most often have a goal in mind, a vision they are seeking to fulfill and are learning how to remove the threads of other spells that would inhibit their realization. In some ways, they may be thought of as the bomb squad of the spirit world able to defuse negative and malicious magic before it goes off.

FEBRUARY 19ᵀᴴ
Ivarthyn: Heart of Gold
MAGIC: SACRED POOL
CONSTELLATION: ATAROLD, MONOCEROS
PLANETARY ASSOCIATION: MERCURY
FAERIE ASSISTANTS: SHABRANG BEHZĀD

Those under this spirit's care have a kind benefactor, indeed, and thus are either learning to be gentle or kind adepts thems'elves or have, by virtue of karma, earned the privilege of studying with this great second ray Master.

Because of this spirit's support, these elves are often very daring and willing to risk a great deal in order to gain much. They are not afraid of being criticized by him, although one does tend to develop an eagerness to please the one who has been so kind and generous. Still, this spirit encourages boldness and his charges seldom disappoint him. Sometimes, this spirit deals with those of a rebellious nature who are in need of a little gentle taming, but he never seeks to break their spirit but rather to guide it toward productive accomplishment.

FEBRUARY 20ᵀᴴ

Soråderfyn: Smells the Weather Changing

MAGIC: SACRED POOL
CONSTELLATION: LUTRA, PISCES
PLANETARY ASSOCIATION: PLUTO
FAERIE ASSISTANTS: SIMURGH

This spirit teaches the understanding of atmosphere both in material climate and emotional and psychological ambience. Those under her tutelage truly know or learn which way the wind is blowing. These elves often develop an interest in weather forecasting or psychology.

These elfin come to achieve the power of endurance; they can put up with a great deal and are willing to sacrifice much to gain what they desire. They can be quite idealistic and will stand true to their beliefs. If they are vegetarian, for instance, they will not eat meat even if it means they will go hungry. They do need to be cautious of becoming fanatical about their beliefs.

FEBRUARY 21ST

Nevynte: On a Whim

MAGIC: FAERY CIRCLE
CONSTELLATION: HOLVORO, FORNAX
PLANETARY ASSOCIATION: MOON
FAERIE ASSISTANTS: HUMA

Nevynte is a whimsical Shining One whose teachings often come unexpectedly and those under her instruction learn that life is ever surprising, that there are presents hidden along the path of life to delight them when they least expect it.

These elves develop a love of life and like to take on new challenges. They are often of an extraverted nature in the sense that they plunge into things without necessarily thinking about what will happen or planning ahead, for they develop an instinctive sense that somehow it will all work out, or if they get in trouble they will just as easily get out of it.

FEBRUARY 22ND

Vänderthe: Touched by Magic

MAGIC: CAULDRON OF REBIRTH
CONSTELLATION: HOLVORO, FORNAX
PLANETARY ASSOCIATION: URANUS
FAERIE ASSISTANTS: HADHAYOSH

Spirituality and revelation are an important part of this spirit's teaching. Those under her influence are prone to feel that life is constantly revealing new things to them and that they encounter a series of peak moments.

However, because such highs cannot be maintained permanently they can have a tendency to manic depression, often feeling let down by those around them that do not share their enthusiasm or optimistic outlook. Therefore, this spirit helps those in her care to moderate their enthusiasm, to keep it at a long roar, so to speak, so they can store and preserve their energy instead of burning it out quickly like a meteor.

FEBRUARY 23ʳᴰ

Zoleyn: Would Love to Dance
MAGIC: SACRED POOL
CONSTELLATION: SARTH, VELA
PLANETARY ASSOCIATION: ASTEROIDS
FAERIE ASSISTANTS: SHAMIR

This spirit loves to dance and views and teaches life as a dance. Those under his care learn grace of movement, elegance of action, and how to develop their unique style. Yet this is not a superfluous action. This spirit teaches one how to express one's inner beauty outwardly so that the expression *what you see is what you get* aptly describes them. And what you will see with these elves as they mature under this spirit's care is a thing of beauty and wonder. For these fae, every action, every movement is magic.

FEBRUARY 24ᵀᴴ

Lothynfe: Magic Maker
MAGIC: THE MAGIC MIRROR
CONSTELLATION: FAERO, TRIANGULUM
PLANETARY ASSOCIATION: URANUS
FAERIE ASSISTANTS: ZIG

This spirit instructs the elves in his care how to make the world work to their advantage, to play by the rules of the world and beat those of the world at their own game. These elves develop a confidence in interacting in the system, but they are also improving their powers of shape shifting for they learn to appear to be whatever individuals expect of them. They even learn how to use people's prejudices and preconceptions to guide and influence their behaviors, which may seem manipulative to some, but which is often necessary in the course of these elves' magical evolution.

February 25th
Qyndarys: Roams the Library

MAGIC: CAULDRON OF REBIRTH
CONSTELLATION: ALDAR, SERPENS
PLANETARY ASSOCIATION: MERCURY
FAERIE ASSISTANTS: URAEUS

The elves who are guided by this Shining One make great researchers. However, they don't simply take what they find and accept it but constantly check what they've learned against practical reality. Therefore, even if they find the most ancient grimoire, they will test its spells and rituals and adjust them as needed for greatest effect. They truly make the old new and re-envision all that they encounter.

These elves often remake things. They tear them apart and put them back together in new ways. They take different objects and combine them making something new and greater. They reinvent the world.

MANY PEOPLE ARE WAITING FOR THE APOLCALYPSE. THE SHINING ONES ARE STRIVING TO AVOID IT.

FEBRUARY 26TH

Hidarve: Good Soul

MAGIC: SPEAR OF LIGHT AND DESTINY
CONSTELLATION: VANUS, VOLANS
PLANETARY ASSOCIATION: MARS
FAERIE ASSISTANTS: HIERACOSPHINX

Hidarve shows those born under her the importance of purity and sincerity. She shows how an open and pure soul becomes free of karma and thus attracts the very best that life can offer and moves one rapidly up the ladder of evolutionary development.

These elves generally have an intense desire for relationship. They sometimes need to learn not simply to have sex but to share their love with those who will truly value it, for their hunger for connection is sometimes taken advantage of by those who don't really care and they at times can pursue sex simply for the momentary connection. Frequently, these elves become tantric adepts.

FEBRUARY 27TH

Feyndrys: Far Away Moon

MAGIC: THE RINGS OF POWER
CONSTELLATION: ELPAN, CAMELOPARDALIS
PLANETARY ASSOCIATION: SUN
FAERIE ASSISTANTS: THREE-LEGGED CROW

The elves born here strive to improve their psychic and intuitive facilities. They see not only what is near but also what is afar. Not that the world is deterministic but their ability to intuit the future from an individual's habits and propensities becomes profound. Because of this ability, they also, with this spirit's help, learn what individuals can do to change their fate and alter the direction of their lives and truly achieve what they desire. Alas, few are prone to listen to the advice of elves, and these fae will have to study under different spirits for their influence to become ever more powerful so their advice is heeded. In time, these fae will become very charismatic beings.

FEBRUARY 28TH

Ynderfor: Will Defend the Forest

MAGIC: CAULDRON OF ABUNDANCE, CORNUCOPIA
CONSTELLATION: GATH, CRUX
PLANETARY ASSOCIATION: PLUTO
FAERIE ASSISTANTS: PETSUCHOS

This spirit teaches that the forest is life; it is the source of wondrous things, of roots, herbs and plants of healing and illumination, the source of oxygen and the friend to all. Those born under this Shining One's influence thus often become protectors of the forest and all things of Nature and crusaders against the extinction of numerous species.

These elves always have a tendency toward love at first sight and when they do, indeed, act to protect Nature, they often find love, for Nature provides. These elfin know the joy of small intimate group action and become very vibrant individuals.

> *WHEN WE ELVES HEAR SOMEONE SAY THEY WISH THEY WERE YOUNG AGAIN, WE THINK, "JUST WAIT!"*

FEBRUARY 29TH

Ibarys: Hangs with the People

MAGIC: SPEAR OF LIGHT AND DESTINY
CONSTELLATION: ARAK, SAGITTARIUS
PLANETARY ASSOCIATION: SATURN
FAERIE ASSISTANTS: BENNU

The elves born under this spirit's auspices move easily among the mass of people and are often found fighting for the rights of minorities. They care about the common people, although elves, even in groups, are never common.

However, these individuals who care so much for others and give so much of thems'elves also need to learn how to retreat and replenish thems'elves. They are developing leadership abilities and like all leaders need a time of reflection so they may hold true to what is right, not merely what is popular.

> *MANY PEOPLE THINK WE ELVES SPEND ALL OUR TIME CELEBRATING. AND THIS IS TRUE IF YOU REALIZE THAT OUR CELEBRATIONS ARE NOT ENTIRELY UNLIKE THE WAY A PRIEST CELEBRATES THE MASS. NOT THAT OUR CELEBRATIONS INVOLVE RITUAL FOR THEY DO NOT NECESSARILY DO SO, BUT THAT OUR CELEBRATIONS ALSO REVEL IN SACRED, MIRACULOUS, AND MAGICAL ASPECTS OF LIFE.*

MARCH

JÅNDURĖL: KNOWS WHAT IS TO COME

MONTH: MARCH

MAGIC: DIVINATION

CONTINENT: CENTRAL AMERICA AND CARIBBEAN ISLANDS

CONSTELLATION: ZILONDAR, URSA MINOR

PLANETARY ASSOCIATION: PLUTO

FAERIE ASSISTANTS: WHITE CADEJO

Jåndurėl is the master of Divination of every sort and inspires humanity in every art designed to speak to the spirit world. She rules the Caribbean and Central America and all who dwell or were born there or whose ancestors come from this region. She understands thoroughly the inner workings of the Universe, but particularly its laws as they function on the Earth and can help one understand the underlying laws or mechanisms that function within Nature.

WHILE THE SHINING ONES GUIDE US, THEY DO NOT COMPEL. THE CHOICE IS EVER OURS AND THEY WOULD NOT INTERFERE WITH OUR MAGIC.

Rivynal: Understands the Hand
MARCH 1ST TO 10TH

MAGIC: CHIROMANCY
AREA: CARIBBEAN ISLANDS
CONSTELLATION: IRANALI, PICTOR
PLANETARY ASSOCIATION: MARS
FAERIE ASSISTANTS: MERMAIDS

This Shining One is a master of Chiromancy or palmistry and can instruct anyone in the secrets of reading the hand. She also is a patron of villages. She favors the idyllic nature of small village life and is particularly found of encouraging community atmosphere. She is further a protector of ancient sites, especially homes, or buildings that are architectural treasures and thus is a patron of preservation societies. The mermaids and water spirits assist her, so any local spring, pond, lake, river or ancient well, which used to be the center of town life, is a magical place for her.

Isal: Card Stirrer
MARCH 11TH TO 20TH

MAGIC: TAROT
AREA: MEXICO
CONSTELLATION: URODELA, LACERTA
PLANETARY ASSOCIATION: SUN
FAERIE ASSISTANTS: CHANEQUE

Isal is the patron of those who use the tarot or other cards for divination including those who use regular playing cards for this purpose. She is also the patron of archeologists and treasure hunters, particularly those who dig for treasure. The Chaneque, the small sprites and nature guardians of Mexico, are her especial helpers. She further has an alliance with griffins and encourages bravery and boldness as well as favoring the valiant. The saying: *Fortune favors the brave*, is a reflection of this spirit's nature.

Piånål: Sorts the Sticks
MARCH 21ST TO 31ST

MAGIC: I CHING
AREA: CENTRAL AMERICA
CONSTELLATION: OLÉLTRE, TELESCOPIUM
PLANETARY ASSOCIATION: URANUS
FAERIE ASSISTANTS: VISION SERPENTS

Piånål is a master of the I Ching and other systems of divination that use sticks to arrive at a result. The Vision Serpents, which are also the Vines of Revelation, are his assistants for he helps those who seek his aid to look into the future and see all that may be. He is also associated with fire dancers and drumming around fires to create a trance atmosphere. Thus he is often found associated with those who do fire spinning. Furthermore, he can teach the magician on the use of fire as a protective as well as evocative power. He teaches the ancient art of Pyromancy to those interested.

MARCH 1ST
Hylåne: Growing Wiser

MAGIC: STAFF OF POWER
CONSTELLATION: ECH, HERCULES
PLANETARY ASSOCIATION:
FAERIE ASSISTANTS: CHANEQUE

As the meaning of her name signifies, this Shining Ones aids those born under Hylåne to grow wiser. Hers is the School for Sages.

Naturally, those under her instruction go through a lot in life. She takes them through a myriad of experiences, some upsetting, many unexpected, that gradually lead her students to gain a wider understanding of their lives and the lives of others and from this experience comes knowledge, understanding and eventually wisdom.

March 2nd

Kelavyn: It was So on Target

Magic: Cauldron of Abundance, Cornucopia
Constellation: Nalon, Corvus
Planetary Association: Mars
Faerie Assistants: Quinametzin

In many ways, those under this spirit's guidance learn economy of effort. They truly come to understand the mechanics of life, the pivotal and fulcrum points and how to get the most from the least. These elves learn to waste nothing. They are very good at accomplishing a great deal with little and often are the ones who have *had to pull thems'elves up by their own bootstraps* as the saying goes. They are often individuals who acquire a great deal, lose it all and then gain it all back again. From these experiences they attain a certainty and a confidence about their ability to always bounce back that not many have in life.

Some elves talk, some elves listen.
Some elves dance until we glisten.

The Shining Ones

MARCH 3ᴿᴰ
Nathanådyn: Nothing Stopping It from Happening

MAGIC: CAULDRON OF REBIRTH
CONSTELLATION: RALTOFRA, CORONA BOREALIS
PLANETARY ASSOCIATION: JUPITER
FAERIE ASSISTANTS: RACUMON

This spirit helps the elfin in his care to become utterly fearless. These elves are not afraid of expressing thems'elves or saying what they think, nor are they afraid of what others think. In fact, they very much look forward to a challenging exchange of ideas and if proven wrong will easily alter or adapt their ideas to a greater and more encompassing understanding. Alas, they sometimes get frustrated with those who are utterly intransigent and those who are unwilling to continue a discussion as soon as it is clear that their own thinking is faulty. These elves are in this lifetime to learn to have some compassion rather than to merely laugh at and make fun of those of inferior intelligence and logical capacity.

MARCH 4ᵀᴴ
Päletha: Protected by the Wind

MAGIC: THE MAGIC MIRROR
CONSTELLATION: HELON, SCUTUM
PLANETARY ASSOCIATION: MERCURY
FAERIE ASSISTANTS: WERE-JAGUAR

This spirit aids those in her care to gain the ability to intellectually understand nearly anyone, even those who are themselves confused in what they believe. Thus these elves see to the heart of nearly any situation or issue for they are developing profound insight into the world in all its forms.

It is these elfin, who have such powerful mental abilities, that come to the understanding of mind over matter and in consequence of this, as they become ever more adept will be able to do things that seem miraculous to others. *They can move mountains*, as the expression goes.

March 5th

Jylåfyn: In the Midst of the Magic

Magic: Sword of Truth and Justice
Constellation: Acantha, Circinus
Planetary Association: Sun
Faerie Assistants: Payatami

The elfin born in this spirit's care tend to be very active beings, who when interested in anything become totally absorbed by that interest. Thus they are prone to obsessions and when this is directed creatively they can accomplish amazing things.

These fae are able to shake up the world. They believe in their own vision with a depth and intensity that affects nearly all around them. They often create and live in their own realms and are quick to set things right if they go wrong. They will not tolerate injustice.

March 6th

Peråvyn: Quiet Eyes

Magic: Cauldron of Abundance, Cornucopia
Constellation: Ånlea, Antlia
Planetary Association: Pluto
Faerie Assistants: Cuarahu-Yara

These fae born here develop the power of inner concentration and focus and with that focus can achieve nearly anything they desire.

The Shining Ones

They like to be recognized for their accomplishments but will give generously to those who appreciate them in turn. They have a powerful drive as individuals and often become leaders in whatever field they enter. This spirit helps them to moderate that power so they do not exhaust thems'elves and their energy, or over stress thems'elves for otherwise they are prone to heart attacks and strokes.

MARCH 7TH

Qåndareal: Redeems the Lost

MAGIC: SWORD OF TRUTH AND JUSTICE
CONSTELLATION: IFOL, LYNX
PLANETARY ASSOCIATION: NEPTUNE
FAERIE ASSISTANTS: YAGUAROGUI

This Shining One is dedicated to helping those who have taken the wrong path to aright thems'elves, begin again and move forward. She helps the Unseelie turn to the Seelie life and in all ways aids those in her care to become karmically free. Those who stay under her guidance often do the same thing, helping those they encounter to develop better life habits, thus you may find these elves pursuing careers as counselors, particularly addiction counselors, or serving as mentors and sponsors for those who are attempting to get their life straight.

WE CALL THEM SHINING ONES BECAUSE THEY GLOW. THEY ARE STARS—BEINGS OF LIGHT.

March 8th
Väsheyn: Tree of Life
Magic: Staff of Power
Constellation: Pavoca, Pavo
Planetary Association: Jupiter
Faerie Assistants: Mixcoatl

Those under this spirit's influence are often attracted to studying the Qabalah, or systems theory, or unified field theories. They want to understand things as a whole and are, of course, meant to do so. They are or will learn to be organizational managers.

These elves tend to become very thorough as individuals. They learn to overlook nothing and see to everything. They become very mature and reliable beings who can attend to many things at once. They are genuine multi-taskers. They are in many ways like a cloud hovering over an area and observing everything.

March 9th
Shålynsa: Silent Thoughts
Magic: Faery Circle
Constellation: Helon, Scutum
Planetary Association: Sun
Faerie Assistants: Xan

Shålynsa teaches the power of thought and thought projection and transference, which is the ability to influence others with one's thoughts without actually saying anything to them out loud. Because of this, these individuals develop a powerful aura and influence their surrounding environment profoundly. At first, of course, their efforts are practiced ones and could be seen as manipulative, but this is just during their training period and as

The Shining Ones

they advance they begin to influence others with no conscious effort to do so. They need do nothing more than show up and be thems'elves.

MARCH 10ᵀᴴ
Sidafyn: Sits Patiently

MAGIC: CAULDRON OF REBIRTH
CONSTELLATION: PUTOR, SCULPTOR
PLANETARY ASSOCIATION: PLUTO
FAERIE ASSISTANTS: XELHUA

Those under this Shining One's influence are in the process of learning faith, and how to wait patiently with an inner certainty that the magic will fulfill itself in time and that interfering with it at certain stages, when it is still gestating, merely makes things take longer to come about.

These individuals are often on the verge of a major ascension in their next life, but have to fulfill this one first and not to do anything that will complicate matters or retard their progress. They have passed the test, now they just have to wait for the new position, assignment or quest they will be given. Learning patience is never a waste of time.

MARCH 11ᵀᴴ
Radånthel: Runs for the Joy of it

MAGIC: THE RINGS OF POWER
CONSTELLATION: WONSA, CASSIOPEIA
PLANETARY ASSOCIATION: NEPTUNE
FAERIE ASSISTANTS: DESANA

Those under this spirit's aegis are often reveling in their newfound

The Silver Elves

power. They are, in many ways, like little children who can't help but want to run and leap about. Radånthel doesn't tell them not to celebrate their achievement, as parents often tell their littles not to run around, but does remind these elves to do so safely for their own sakes as well as that of others. In time, of course, they will go beyond celebration into plunging into the new work that is before them. For now, however, they have achieved and are meant to enjoy their success.

MARCH 12ᵀᴴ
Cabryniyl: Makes a Place for Those as Yet Unborn
MAGIC: FAERY CIRCLE
CONSTELLATION: RALTOFRA, CORONA BOREALIS
PLANETARY ASSOCIATION: MOON
FAERIE ASSISTANTS: HADEWA

This spirit heals elfin who are recently awakened and naturally also has under his care those who are dedicated to awakening others. These elfin tend to be extremely passionate beings and since awakening itself can be a profound moment of psychological realization they carry that feeling within thems'elves nearly always. This experience often brings about tears of joy and relief and these elfin become adept at nurturing those who are going through this critical phase of spiritual development.

> *SOME PEOPLE THINK THE SHINING ONES ARE PART OF A VAST CONSPIRACY. THEY ARE. IT'S CALLED EVOLUTION!*

MARCH 13TH

Ikynver: Have Guided Me Always
MAGIC: HORN OF CALLING
CONSTELLATION: FAERO, TRIANGULUM
PLANETARY ASSOCIATION: SATURN
FAERIE ASSISTANTS: QUEL

The fae born here have a strong sense of their connection to the spirit world and often seek to enhance their understanding of that world and the rules, laws, and modes with which it is ordered. They are serious students of the occult and seek to know and master the hidden forces that control life. They have a great propensity to attract others of a similar nature. These elfin begin to plant seeds of magic that will develop later. They are long-term planners and think in terms of generations and aeons not just in days or years.

MARCH 14TH

Nidynfe: Once Is Not Enough
MAGIC: SPEAR OF LIGHT AND DESTINY
CONSTELLATION: HOLVORO, FORNAX
PLANETARY ASSOCIATION: MERCURY
FAERIE ASSISTANTS: WERE-COYOTE

These elfin born here are true lovers of life. They do not lead life unwillingly nor spend their precious time complaining about every obstacle they may encounter but embrace life fully and with a fervor that is astounding to others. They are truly filled with spirit and other folks feel more confident just from being around them. There is something about these elves that just makes one feel like smiling and there are few who meet them that do not instantly like them, although they may not be able to say exactly why. Others very eagerly pitch in if ever these elfin seem to need help.

March 15th

Urdyndre: Their Own Voice

MAGIC: SPEAR OF LIGHT AND DESTINY
CONSTELLATION: IRANALI, PICTOR
PLANETARY ASSOCIATION: URANUS
FAERIE ASSISTANTS: HOH

Urdyndre helps individuals to find their own voice, to speak eloquently for thems'elves and to express their ideas and experiences in a unique and powerful fashion. Those just beginning under this spirit's guidance often struggle to express thems'elves, feel pent up and in particular unable to express their feelings. But in the course of time these become great masters of communication who not only write or speak clearly but also do so with a grace and power that is deeply moving to others.

March 16th

Izynde: Helps the Worthy

MAGIC: SHIELD OF LOVE AND PROTECTION
CONSTELLATION: ÅNLEA, ANTLIA
PLANETARY ASSOCIATION: ASTEROIDS
FAERIE ASSISTANTS: BALAM-QUITZE

This spirit only aids those who have earned the privilege of her aid. If you were born here, you have probably done much to gain this right. You have prepared for this lifetime, worked hard for it and have earned it. And having done so you are now under the protection of this spirit who will alter your life to move you toward those experiences that are significant for you. If you feel that someone is moving your life at times from above, you are surely right. If you don't feel worthy of this attention from the spirits, you will come to do so and gain a sense of the significance of your life. If you feel you are overly restrained, know that this is for your own good to get you where you need be for continued development of our spirit, soul and powers.

March 17th

Talåleyn: Soulful Healing

MAGIC: STAFF OF POWER
CONSTELLATION: FYR, VULPECULA
PLANETARY ASSOCIATION: ASTEROIDS
FAERIE ASSISTANTS: ITZPAPALOTL

Because this spirit deals with soulful healing, those under her care often find careers in counseling, particularly spiritual counseling, couple counseling and so on. This life will bring healing to their own souls, to their relationships and their ability to maintain relationship.

These elfin often feel like the floodgates have opened unto their feelings and they are, at times, overwhelmed by the intensity of what they experience. Much of what has long been repressed is freed within them, and they begin to embrace life with intensity. This lifetime for these fae is often like one of ice gradually melting and flowing forth where it will.

SOME SAY PATIENCE IS A VIRTUE. ELVES CALL IT A MAGIC.

MARCH 18TH

Woveryl: Warrior of the Way

MAGIC: SPEAR OF LIGHT AND DESTINY

CONSTELLATION: FADRON, PERSEUS

PLANETARY ASSOCIATION: MOON

FAERIE ASSISTANTS: ACALICA

The elfin under the instruction of this spirit are learning to be warriors for truth and justice in the world. They are or become extremely determined beings and will not shirk death if need be to protect or obtain what they feel to be right.

Because of this, these fae are often seen as extremely attractive. This is not necessarily due to any physical features but because of their incredible courage and daring. They are sometimes seen as the "bad" boy or girl type, although their dedication is not about mere rebellion but about truly setting things right in the world.

MARCH 19TH

Naelvyn: New Way to Go

MAGIC: CAULDRON OF REBIRTH

CONSTELLATION: IRANALI, PICTOR

PLANETARY ASSOCIATION: NEPTUNE

FAERIE ASSISTANTS: HOHOTTU

Naelvyn offers new alternatives to those in his care, revealing new possibilities and ways of being in the world. This is a new life on a higher level for these elfin and much may feel unfamiliar about the world, and many of these elfin feel as though they are aliens in the world and they often don't relate to the idea of being human at all.

Because they are new to the world, so to speak, these fae often go through a period of attempting to stabilize thems'elves in the world, to familiarize thems'elves and establish thems'elves, which leads these elfin to eventual success in the world and in their chosen careers.

MARCH 20TH

Breånfe: Beyond Belief

MAGIC: THE RINGS OF POWER
CONSTELLATION: RYSTATA, CAELUM
PLANETARY ASSOCIATION: MARS
FAERIE ASSISTANTS: JAMAINA

This Shining One introduces her protégés to fantastic possibilities and a more expansive understanding of the world and the Universe. In learning from her, these elfin begin to transcend the limitations of this dimension and act and function under more powerful and encompassing laws of the Universe.

This gives these fae a sense of newfound freedom. Many of the karmic limitations that had inhibited them previously are lifted in this lifetime and they can do and accomplish a great deal more than they could previously. In many ways, they feel like a whole world of revelation is opened to them, they can glimpse into the Akashic Record or otherwise are privy to information to which most folks have no access.

> *ELVES COME TOGETHER AND SEPARATE AS EASILY AS WATER, SAVE WE EVER CARRY THE MEMORY OF OUR UNION IN OUR HEARTS.*

March 21st

Grodål: From Another Dimension

MAGIC: CAULDRON OF ABUNDANCE, CORNUCOPIA

CONSTELLATION: ARAK, SAGITTARIUS

PLANETARY ASSOCIATION: SATURN

FAERIE ASSISTANTS: TEZCATLIPOCA

These elfin are often volunteers from other dimensions who have come to help or have chosen this world to learn a particular lesson that will be helpful to them in the future. Sometimes this transference is confusing at first and it may take time for them to adapt to this new and strange world.

These elfin often feel vulnerable in this unfamiliar world and are not always sure how to react to unfamiliar feelings, settings and situations. However, this Shining One will do all in his power to help them acclimate and achieve what they have come here to accomplish.

March 22nd

Leŏnde: Lady of the Rivers

MAGIC: FAERY CIRCLE

CONSTELLATION: SACRO, CRATER

PLANETARY ASSOCIATION: MERCURY

FAERIE ASSISTANTS: BOCHICA

Leŏnde teaches the magic of feelings, of connections and of the ability to flow ever on. Those under her guidance truly learn to *go with the flow*.

These elfin are subject to make sudden transformations in their lives based on an unexpected change of ideas, feelings or circumstances. They are often said to *turn on a dime*. Thus they can seem very unpredictable beings. However, it is also true that until these fae learn to go with flow that these sudden changes will occur outwardly in their lives, leading them to scramble to keep things going. However, as they learn the lessons of this spirit they will increasingly be the masters of the change rather than feel they are its victims.

March 23rd

Widarfyn: Wanders in Their Dreams

Magic: Shield of Love and Protection
Constellation: Fadron, Perseus
Planetary Association: Jupiter
Faerie Assistants: Utiu

Those under this spirit's guidance learn the power of dreams, lucid dreaming and ultimately learn to appear in other's dreams or to live in the dream world, which is to say use the dream world to step from one dimension to another.

Because of their advanced understanding of the nature of reality, these elfin are often seen as being transformative and innovative thinkers, for their thinking is greatly informed by their dreams and their imaginal capacity. They easily affect others who are impressed by the uniqueness of their being.

> THE SHINING ONES KNOW US BETTER THAN ANYONE. THUS, THOSE WHO TRUST THEM AND THOSE WHO DON'T USUALLY HAVE GOOD REASONS FOR DOING SO.

March 24th

Hidareyl: Telling Tales in the Glen

MAGIC: SACRED POOL
CONSTELLATION: RYND, EQUULEUS
PLANETARY ASSOCIATION: MERCURY
FAERIE ASSISTANTS: TLOTLI

This Shining One is a great mentor for storytellers of all sorts, fiction writers, memoir writers and raconteurs. At the same time, these elves often love fiction, good writing and eloquent expression.

These elfin may create the atmosphere and ambience of elven homes. They are frequently the ones that help awaken the inner elf through their fiction. In some ways, these fae create worlds, homes, communities that, while they only seem to exist in fiction at this point, find a place in the hearts and minds of other elfin. They make Faerie real in our imaginations and we feel called to make the dream real in our own lives.

March 25th

Teåvyn: Spreading Hope

MAGIC: SPEAR OF LIGHT AND DESTINY
CONSTELLATION: MATH, PYXIS
PLANETARY ASSOCIATION: ASTEROIDS
FAERIE ASSISTANTS: KINICH AHAU

The elfin who act under this Shining One's aegis are out to spread the word, to awaken elves and make Faerie/Elfin real in the world. These often have pixie ancestry and are frequently referred to as *go-getters*.

Because of their drive and passionate natures, these fae can be very warm as individuals, by which we mean they can be physically like furnaces. Sometimes, those under this spirit's guidance are those who have been so buffeted and battered by life that they have nearly given up. However, others of their kind are seeking them and will renew their hope, or reawaken their fire, once they find them.

MARCH 26TH

Glorlelyn: Forever Kin

MAGIC: THE STONE OF THE LAND
CONSTELLATION: URMA, DORADO
PLANETARY ASSOCIATION: MERCURY
FAERIE ASSISTANTS: KEYEME

Glorlelyn teaches that kinship and friendship are the keys to Faerie and the means of making Faerie real in the world. These come to understand that it is not a matter of establishing a nation called Elfin, but a matter of awakening a group of individuals who truly know thems'elves to be kin.

These elves become determined individuals who do all they can to establish and support their kindred in the world. It is not that they don't know the importance of establishing elfin communities, and they often strive to do this, but they are aware that no community will succeed and endure if the feeling of love and connection is not strong within it.

THE ELVES EVER HOPE FOR THE BEST, PLAN FOR THE WORST, AND ACT TOWARD THE POSSIBLE.

MARCH 27TH

Åturyn: As the Stars Shine upon You

MAGIC: THE MAGIC MIRROR

CONSTELLATION: HELON, SCUTUM

PLANETARY ASSOCIATION: SATURN

FAERIE ASSISTANTS: MUDO

Under this spirit's guidance, the pixies born here come to understand the realms of the Shining Ones and the significance of their associations with them. These elves tend to become star enchanters and this spirit will surely help them in learning anything they wish about this ancient art. They may thus similarly have in interest in astrology, astronomy or anything that has to do with the star fields.

These fae often go unrecognized for most of their lives or in their careers only to suddenly gain prominence after years of hard work. It may seem to those on the outside that they appeared out of nowhere, but these elfin know the years of foundational effort that went into their accomplishment.

MARCH 28TH

Ymlefyn: Wide Smile

MAGIC: FAERY CIRCLE

CONSTELLATION: ÅNLEA, ANTLIA

PLANETARY ASSOCIATION: EARTH

FAERIE ASSISTANTS: ALUX NAGUAL

Ymlefyn teaches the power of optimism and the power of an open and free association with others. Will Roger's saying that he *never met a man he didn't like* (we expect that went for women as well) is much in keeping with this spirit's point of view. These elfin learn how to make friends with everyone. The word *like* in this case is not referring so much to a reaction or response to others, but rather an active and determined technique of magic.

These fae usually develop a powerful sense of public taste and fashion; know what will be popular and succeed in the world; and are likely to be ahead of, or creating, upcoming fads. They tend to be very generous and giving individuals who actively nurture all those around them.

MARCH 29TH

Leåvoryn: Longs for the Truth

MAGIC: SHIELD OF LOVE AND PROTECTION
CONSTELLATION: WAND, MICROSCOPIUM
PLANETARY ASSOCIATION: MERCURY
FAERIE ASSISTANTS: TZITZIMIT

Leåvoryn teaches the importance of truth and the need for establishing the facts in every situation. Many under her guidance become scientists seeking to know what makes the world function as it does.

These elfin often challenge conventional wisdom. However, they need to be sure that in finding what they believe to be the truth that they remain open to further information, new data, and other possibilities. Leåvoryn helps them do this. They must be careful not to overthrow one view merely to establish another that is equally intransigent.

> THE ELVES SAY A STAR IS THE HOME OF BILLIONS OF SHINING ONES DANCING TOGETHER.

March 30th

Våvynde: Tree Dweller

Magic: Horn of Calling
Constellation: Ånlea, Antlia
Planetary Association: Mercury
Faerie Assistants: La Mojana

This spirit teaches the importance of harmony with nature, particularly the significance of our tree friends, and how we will in time carry the trees into space. These elfin learn to relate to the trees as sentient beings, to respect their lives, and to understand the beauty of their deep wisdom as well as the fact that many of them are active benefactors to us and many other species.

Because of this increased understanding of the sentient nature of life, these fae are also able to sympathize with a wide range of individuals although they are often frustrated by those who kill the trees so callously without thought to the welfare of the trees or the world.

March 31st

Ålynfar: Allays the Pain

Magic: The Magic Mirror
Constellation: Arandus, Reticulum
Planetary Association: Saturn
Faerie Assistants: Duende

This Shining One helps those under his influence to learn empathy and to use it to soothe the pain and suffering of others. Thus these fae tend to be healers, nurses, doctors, therapists or find an interest or career in any field that aids others to endure and overcome suffering.

The Shining Ones

These elfin often become shamanic healers who deal not only with the body but the psyche of the individual under their care and will go into the netherworlds to find the source of their pain and the cure for it. They develop tremendous will power and learn how to remove other's suffering without taking it on thems'elves. These become truly powerful Curanderos.

> *IF YOU WISH TO FIND THE ELVES IN ANY SOCIETY, YOU NEED LOOK LITTLE FURTHER THAN THE ARTISTS, THE DREAMERS, AND THE EXPLORERS.*

> *DO ELVES MAKE CLAIM TO EVERY THING GOOD IN THE WORLD? YES, BUT WE'RE ALWAYS EAGER TO SHARE.*

> THE SHINING ONES EXIST THROUGHOUT THE UNIVERSE, WEAVING STARLIGHT TO UPLIFT ALL.

> THE ELVES NOT ONLY HAVE DREAM CATCHERS IN THEIR HOMES, BUT ALSO DREAM LIBERATORS AS WELL.

> THOUGHTS EXIST IN AN OCEAN OF MIND. WHEN WE ELVES SEEK INSPIRATION, WE GO SWIMMING IN OUR IMAGINATIONS.

April

Hylyntheyl: Calls to the Ancient Ones

Month: April

Magic: Necroturgy

Continent: North America

Constellation: Salmo, Pisces Austrinus

Planetary Association: Moon

Faerie Assistants: Deer People

This Shining One is assisted by the deer people and oversees the evolution of North America and those living or born upon it. She is an expert at Necroturgy that is using the power of the past, of tradition, to influence the present. She has a connection to all the ancient Gods and Goddesses of the Earth, the forgotten Gods, the ones remembered but no longer worshipped, and the Shining Ones who have moved beyond this dimension, and she can help one communicate with and gain guidance and power from them and with the Ancestors of the Land.

Everyone looks at the world from where they are standing at the moment.
—Old Elven Saying

Farynal: Bringing Light to Darkness
APRIL 1ST TO 10TH
MAGIC: NECROMANCY

AREA: CANADA AND ALASKA

CONSTELLATION: SETÅTRU, OPHIUCUS

PLANETARY ASSOCIATION: MOON

FAERIE ASSISTANTS: ALOM-BAG-WINNO-SIS

Farynal, assisted by the Alom-bag-winno-sis who are somewhat prankster-ish water sprites, rules the power of Necromancy, the evocation of the dead for communication. He is thus a patron of Historians. It is important to understand, however, that in contacting the dead, if they are not recently passed, that one is communing with the shard or left over memories or energy radiations/impressions of those spirits who have already gone on to new lives. This and more will be revealed by Farynal, who will also reveal to one many secrets of the past that one can use for success in their current life, as well as guide one to see their own previous incarnations.

Nedånfal: From Life to Life
APRIL 11TH TO 20TH
MAGIC: BARDO MASTER

AREA: WESTERN U.S.

CONSTELLATION: FOCIDA, CHAMALEON

PLANETARY ASSOCIATION: VENUS

FAERIE ASSISTANTS: CANOTILA

This Shining One is assisted by the Canotila: the forest dwelling elves and faeries of America. She also helps one progress from one life to another or to become a master of guiding others in the process of leaving one body and finding another, or moving to a higher dimension of evolution. This is an immensely powerful being and is on the level of what one might call a Dragon, teaching the great secrets involved with death and re-incarnation. These are profound mysteries that are at the heart of what goes on concerning this plane of being and any who truly understand her teachings automatically rise to a more profound level of developmental being.

Jidyndal: Evokes the Ancestors
APRIL 21ST TO 30TH
MAGIC: ANCESTORURGY
AREA: EASTERN U.S.
CONSTELLATION: ORMYN, CENTAURUS
PLANETARY ASSOCIATION: PLUTO
FAERIE ASSISTANTS: MISI-KINEPIKW

The Misi-kinepikw are horned serpents that assist Jidyndal to teach the magician how to conjure and use the power of tradition and particularly the Collective Unconscious of hir personal ancestry as a great magical power. The serpent symbolizes knowledge, particularly magical or esoteric knowledge, and the horns represent power, strength and maturity, thus these are very ancient and potent allies. With this Shining One's aid one can connect to the power of the Shining Ones and create wondrous magic.

APRIL 1ST

Gylavyn: From the Dreamtime
MAGIC: CAULDRON OF REBIRTH
CONSTELLATION: EQALO, CETUS
PLANETARY ASSOCIATION: ASTEROIDS
FAERIE ASSISTANTS: FIRE DRAGONS

Gylavyn helps the elfin born under her auspices to understand the formative powers of life found in the Dreamtime from which all has manifested into the material world. These elves connect to the first powers, the first peoples and come to understand how the Universe and the world came to be.

These fae often get a glimpse, in a moment of incredible clarity, of what life is all about and see in an instant the direction of their lives and attain their Visions for fulfilling their purpose in life. They are able to connect to their higher spiritual s'elves and thus can become powerful magi or spiritual leaders.

April 2nd

Keravyn: Joy of Loving

Magic: The Stone of the Land
Constellation: Pavoca, Pavo
Planetary Association: Mars
Faerie Assistants: Ishigaq

These elfin learn the power of joy, of love and of empowering others. They tend to become radiant beings who easily affect any environment that they may find thems'elves in.

Although the source of their power is one of joyous action, these elfin develop a powerful optimistic view of life for without the power of mind their joy would soon be overwhelmed by the negative thoughts and ideas that tend to bombard one continually in this world. Some might think these fae naïve, or simply ignoring reality, but in fact they have set their minds on their individual Vision and hold true to it despite all attempts to dissuade them of its infeasibility. They will in the course of time be proven correct in their advanced thinking.

APRIL 3ʳᴰ

Jiveryn: I Wish for a Better World

MAGIC: THE RINGS OF POWER
CONSTELLATION: LATUR, INDUS
PLANETARY ASSOCIATION: SUN
FAERIE ASSISTANTS: RAIN BIRD

The elfin under this spirit's care are learning to have faith in the future. They often endure great trials in life but come to understand the cycles of life and are assured by this spirit that in time the reward for all their efforts will come. Thus these are learning to hold on to, and be true to, their dreams.

These elfin often have a tendency to let thems'elves be buffeted by life, tossed here and there by changing circumstance and seem up or down according to this or that mood or event. Thus in this lifetime, they are gradually developing a steadiness of character that will carry them through the vicissitudes of life so they eventually become the buoy to which others cling in difficult times.

APRIL 4ᵀᴴ

Jynvalyn: Inner Realization

MAGIC: HORN OF CALLING
CONSTELLATION: LEPGAR, CAPRICORNUS
PLANETARY ASSOCIATION: SUN
FAERIE ASSISTANTS: AGLOOLIK

Those born under this spirit's care often feel that they have been Called and have a particular quest or destiny to fulfill and will wait their entire lives for the moment to arrive when they are contacted by those they sense are destined to awakened them.

Once they feel they have received this Call or experienced this awakening, they become very dedicated and devoted individuals pursuing with great energy the fulfillment of whatever they perceive their mission to be and usually seeking others to help them do so.

April 5th

Suarfyn: So Much More to It

MAGIC: FAERY CIRCLE
CONSTELLATION: FOCIDA, CHAMALEON
PLANETARY ASSOCIATION: MOON
FAERIE ASSISTANTS: GANDAYAH

Suarfyn reveals to the elfin under her guidance that there is more, ever more to learn, develop and do. She often provides the Elfae (elfin-faerie folk) with a glimpse into the vast realm of possibilities, long enough so they get a sense of all that can be, but brief enough so they are not overwhelmed.

These elfin often gain great power over the elements and the elementals and can accomplish amazing things. They are farsighted and apply the lessons of the past to the future, knowing that these are reflective in many ways of each other.

April 6th

Leshynde: Lost Treasure

MAGIC: SWORD OF TRUTH AND JUSTICE
CONSTELLATION: FOLI, LYRA
PLANETARY ASSOCIATION: ASTERIODS
FAERIE ASSISTANTS: GAHONGA

These fae are often seen as old-fashioned since they tend to value virtues, such as nobility, honor and integrity that are often forgotten, ignored or scorned in the modern world. They become aware that these virtues are powers that can be used to great magical effect. Others often look upon these elfin as being limited beings hampered by their old fashioned values, but these values enable these elfin to remain at the center of the storm when all around them are in upheaval. This spirit can also help to find lost treasure and thus treasure hunters often seek her aid.

April 7th

Eterethel: Earth Magic

MAGIC: SHIELD OF LOVE AND PROTECTION
CONSTELLATION: MATH, PYXIS
PLANETARY ASSOCIATION: JUPITER
FAERIE ASSISTANTS: ODHOWS

These elfin learn Earth magic under this spirit's guidance, learn to connect to the old god forms, the Ancient Ones of the Earth and also how to use their power to protect thems'elves and others from the negative forces that have long sought to undo evolutionary progress on the Earth. Often these fae become interested in and quite adept at connecting to the ley lines of the Earth and can thus evoke powerful forces to aid them in their work.

They are particularly able to connect to the waterways of the Earth and thus become deeply psychic beings, imaginative in nature and able to connect easily with other sensitive individuals.

> *FOR MOST ELVES, MEMORIES OF ELFIN ARE NOT SO MUCH THOUGHTS OR IMAGES BUT FEELINGS OF KINSHIP THAT WASH OVER OUR BEINGS LIKE MUSIC.*

April 8th

Resånåle: Seeks Faerie

MAGIC: THE RINGS OF POWER

CONSTELLATION: MADON LUPRAE, CANIS MINOR

PLANETARY ASSOCIATION: VENUS

FAERIE ASSISTANTS: WUCHOWSEN

The fae under this spirit's influence increasingly come to understand how to connect with and obtain the magical powers of Faerie. They will be dream and wish fulfillers who can bring great happiness to others and help others achieve their dreams.

These elves become amazingly flexible as individuals, open-minded and receptive but it is exactly this receptivity that enables them to influence others for they thems'elves are ever perceived as being open and others are encouraged to be the same in response to them. They are often chance takers and at the same time tend to be very lucky.

April 9th

Jyndrynde: Incites Their Spirits

MAGIC: SPEAR OF LIGHT AND DESTINY

CONSTELLATION: LEPGAR, CAPRICORNUS

PLANETARY ASSOCIATION: SUN

FAERIE ASSISTANTS: RAINBOW CROW

This Shining One shows those under his care how to get others enthused, to motivate them toward action, and to fill them with a sense, and power, of spirit.

These elfin develop the ability to recognize what others want or desire and how to attach that desire to the fulfillment of their Vision, showing the individual how they will achieve all they need and have always wanted if they just believe and act with faith. This can be a power that is easily abused so these elfae are usually very mature and evolved spirits, and yet even then the temptation exists and must be mastered. They are here to learn to do what they do for the benefit of all.

APRIL 10TH

Vorasel: Understands the Land

MAGIC: SPEAR OF LIGHT AND DESTINY
CONSTELLATION: FADON LUPRAE, CANIS MAJOR
PLANETARY ASSOCIATION: PLUTO
FAERIE ASSISTANTS: WANA-GAMES-AK

The elfin under this spirit's guidance make great farmers, gardeners, or stewards of the land. They learn to understand what makes the land prosper and flourish. They have or come to have the proverbial green thumb.

Because of this association with growing things, these elves also tend to become health conscious and can find careers or demonstrate interest in nutrition, herbal studies and other things related to a healthy diet. They also have the propensity to become great chefs and understand that food preparation is a great and fundamental magic.

> YOU CAN DESCRIBE THE RELATIONSHIP BETWEEN THE ELVES AND THE SHINING ONES AS BEING SPIRITUAL BUT IT WOULD BE MORE ACCURATE TO DESCRIBE IT AS AFFECTIONATE.

April 11th

Chididyn: Call of the Ancients

MAGIC: SACRED POOL
CONSTELLATION: VERPA, HYDRA
PLANETARY ASSOCIATION: ASTEROIDS
FAERIE ASSISTANTS: ANI HYUNTIKWALASKI

Chididyn helps those in his care to connect to their ancestors, not just their direct ancestors, but the ancestors of their magical race. Thus for elves and faerie folk this means connecting with the energy of the Ancient Sidhe and other Fair Folk. This in part involves delving into the Collective Unconscious of our Peoples.

Because of this connection to the Ancients, these elfin often feel, and indeed are, blessed and protected. They can have the most amazing luck when they least expect it and even when things go poorly for them they ever have a chance at a new beginning.

April 12th

Rafena: Rush of Energy

MAGIC: HORN OF CALLING
CONSTELLATION: IRANALI, PICTOR
PLANETARY ASSOCIATION: ASTEROIDS
FAERIE ASSISTANTS: MISHIPESHU

These elfin are often very enthusiastic participants in anything they join. They are ready to get going, to help out and to make things the best they can be and they convey this positive spirit to those around them.

They learn to be very fair-minded individuals and would do very well as judges of any sort because they develop the capacity to view things impartially and without prejudice and at the same time with a sympathetic and compassionate understanding of circumstances. They don't want to know only what happened, but why it happened. They give everyone a fair hearing.

APRIL 13TH
Irelålys: Heals with Love
MAGIC: CAULDRON OF ABUNDANCE, CORNUCOPIA
CONSTELLATION: ATAROLD, MONOCEROS
PLANETARY ASSOCIATION: MARS
FAERIE ASSISTANTS: GAASYENDIETHA

Irelålys teaches the power of generosity and abundance and those guided by him come to understand the value of giving gifts and tokens of appreciation. These fae learn to always bring a gift when visiting, but the greatest gift they bring, along with the token object, is their true appreciation.

These fae come to sense when it is time to leave any situation. They become so adept at this that they are never there when trouble comes, having already moved on. They never outstay their welcome and they gradually develop an aura of mystery about them.

APRIL 14TH
Zylathys: Yearns for Elfin
MAGIC: SWORD OF TRUTH AND JUSTICE
CONSTELLATION: ECH, HERCULES
PLANETARY ASSOCIATION: JUPITER
FAERIE ASSISTANTS: ONNOINT

Zylathys draws to her those who hunger to make Elfin/Faerie real upon the Earth. These elves struggle for the recognition and acceptance of our kind, often they do this indirectly by fighting for gay rights, woman's rights or the rights of some other minority.

These elfin learn to bear suffering, to remain positive and seemingly unaffected on the outside while transmuting pain within. That is instead of buying into the pecking order where they pick on those beneath them to allay the suffering they have endured, they grin and bear it and thus transform it from suffering to energetic determination and power.

April 15th

Norifyn: Only Wish to Bring Happiness

Magic: Sacred Pool
Constellation: Zilondar, Ursa Minor
Planetary Association: Sun
Faerie Assistants: Were-Cougar

The fae under this Shining One's influence come to learn to be dedicated servers, seeking to help all they encounter and particularly those of the frasorities (fraternity + sorority) they participate in. These elfin are often members of the Great White Lodge and frequently come to study the Blue Books of Alice Bailey.

These come to understand the laws that govern the Universe and the hierarchy of evolutionary development that arises from these laws. Their place in that hierarchy depends upon their own particular level of maturity and dedication but these elves come to see that the only way to heal the world is to help those in it.

> *Some think the Shining Ones are dragons and there is surely a poetic truth in that.*

APRIL 16TH

Irafyn: Heals the Body
MAGIC: THE MAGIC MIRROR
CONSTELLATION: DEOSA, CANCER
PLANETARY ASSOCIATION: MOON
FAERIE ASSISTANTS: EMOGOALEKC

This spirit teaches healing, but especially of the physical body, and those under his influence make good doctors, massage therapists, or others who deal with healing of the body.

These fae develop a close association and empathy with others, and have or learn to have a great bedside manner. Those who come to these elfin for healing love their personalities, and feel a deep rapport with them, as well as a trust and confidence in their healing ability.

APRIL 17TH

Ivyndryl: Helps Others on the Way
MAGIC: HORN OF CALLING
CONSTELLATION: JUFI, OCTANS
PLANETARY ASSOCIATION: MERCURY
FAERIE ASSISTANTS: KACHINA

These elfin are dedicated assistants to others on the path. They are active in awakening others and in helping them get their feet firmly on the spiritual path. They are being prepared for advancement into the realms of the Shining Ones.

With this spirit's aid and the gratitude of those they've helped, these elfae obtain superhuman force and powers that they will be able to wield in future lifetimes. They also learn to use shock tactics to arouse the inner nature of those who are particularly recalcitrant. These are not your average folks, and they play by higher rules.

April 18th

Vayldyn: Tree Shaper
MAGIC: STAFF OF POWER
CONSTELLATION: PAVOCA, PAVO
PLANETARY ASSOCIATION: MARS
FAERIE ASSISTANTS: PAMOLA

Vayldyn teaches those under his influence how to shape their lives and the circumstances of their lives, changing the world around them. These are advancing elfin who will gain more and more power through this lifetime.

These fae develop profound powers of mind and logic, tend to be very thorough in their actions and see to all that needs to be done. They are moving up in the hierarchy of responsibility and attain the ability to oversee great areas of influence and to supervise and nurture increasing numbers of souls thus changing and shaping their lives.

April 19th

Lusånda: Makes It All Right
MAGIC: THE MAGIC MIRROR
CONSTELLATION: ARANDUS, RETICULUM
PLANETARY ASSOCIATION: MOON
FAERIE ASSISTANTS: UNK CEKULA

Lusånda teaches problem-solving and those under her auspices learn the means to make all things work out well. They are ever seeking the keys and the solutions to every situation, the magic formula that will enable all things to turn out as they should and as they intend or as is needed.

These elfin seldom evoke the unconventional; rather they are ever aware of the preconceptions and expectations of those around them and use these basic assumptions to lead those they help from the known and accepted into the realms of the unknown in a step-by-step fashion. They do not violate the norm but use it as the basis for their magic. They make the unusual, understandable.

April 20th
Drodånådyn: Dark Wonder

Magic: Faery Circle
Constellation: Toloto, Carina
Planetary Association: Neptune
Faerie Assistants: Sint Holo

This Shining One introduces one to the mysteries, to the unknown and the unexplained. With his help the elfin begins to see the value of opposition, the good that exists even in those who do evil, and how to arouse the spiritual in those who seem utterly mundane.

These fae seldom conform to the norm in fashion, dress or lifestyle. They are not evil beings, nor do they do evil, but they often are seen as violating convention. They become powerful, determined beings, whose influence alters the way the world views things, and while they may not be accepted at first, their contributions are eventually incorporated and absorbed by traditional society.

> *THE ELVES BELIEVE THE MORE WE SHARE, THE MORE WE HAVE.*

April 21st
Pëlale: Quick Change
MAGIC: CAULDRON OF ABUNDANCE, CORNUCOPIA
CONSTELLATION: WAND, MICROSCOPIUM
PLANETARY ASSOCIATION: SUN
FAERIE ASSISTANTS: HAIETLIK

This Shining One teaches flexibility and adaptability to those born under her aegis, and if they don't value change they will suffer greatly until making and mastering changes is second nature to them. Once they do master this ability, however, their life will be increasingly filled with abundance.

This does not mean that one is bound willy-nilly to their circumstance, but rather these elfin learn to be a few steps ahead of the game, so they are making changes before they are needed instead of ever being forced to transform against their will and thus subject and victim to the vagaries of fate and circumstance.

April 22nd
Yndresa: Willing to Show the Way
MAGIC: SWORD OF TRUTH AND JUSTICE
CONSTELLATION: TARUNTUS, HYDRUS
PLANETARY ASSOCIATION: NEPTUNE
FAERIE ASSISTANTS: AWES-KON-WA

This spirit shows how a righteous life creates good karma, how right livelihood promotes spiritual success and how one can lead a magical, spiritual and successful life in the world.

The elfin under this Shining One's influence learn how to curb temptation with right action, how to replace negative thoughts with positive ones and how acting for what is right and fair for others

The Shining Ones

benefits all of us. These fae learn that service and s'elf interest are not mutually exclusive and in fact work best when combined.

APRIL 23ʳᴰ
Udarfe: Talks to the Trees

MAGIC: FAERY CIRCLE
CONSTELLATION: TONENYS, PUPPIS
PLANETARY ASSOCIATION: ASTEROIDS
FAERIE ASSISTANTS: POK-WEJEE-MEN

Udarfe teaches the language of Nature, how to communicate with any creature or living being and how to make alliances and thus gain assistance from them. One will be able to understand the babbling brook, the tittering birds and the aroma of flowers.

These elves are also learning how to let Nature energize and heal them, replenish their energy and their spirit and thus you often find these fae exploring in the wild, hiking, rock climbing or otherwise pursuing careers that bring them in frequent contact with Nature.

APRIL 24ᵀᴴ
Sålynve: Sharing the Hope

MAGIC: STAFF OF POWER
CONSTELLATION: LEPGAR, CAPRICORNUS
PLANETARY ASSOCIATION: NEPTUNE
FAERIE ASSISTANTS: CANOTILA

This Shining One helps inspire those under her guidance with hope and the power of a utopian outlook. Often this inspiration comes in the form of fiction or fantasy, which are her tools, thus those who aspire to be writers or creators of fantasy do well under her care. She teaches the art of Grammarye.

These elves tend to be torchbearers. They lead the way and inspire others by their courage and endurance. They can be fierce in pursing their goals and show great fortitude in confronting the negativity of the world.

APRIL 25TH

Sovyndre: So Much Rain Clears the Air

MAGIC: SWORD OF TRUTH AND JUSTICE
CONSTELLATION: RAGOL, VIRGO
PLANETARY ASSOCIATION: EARTH
FAERIE ASSISTANTS: PIASA

This spirit brings relief from tension in one's life and in the course of her instruction the elfin feels not only that things will or are getting better, but also that sHe is able to handle any situation and bring clarity to it.

These elfin are subject to brainstorms, sudden revelations and bursts of enlightenment. They further learn to cause such reactions in others that is to say they evoke inspiration in those around them and are therefore perceived as being inspiring individuals. Because of this, they are often seen as being both weird and brilliant.

APRIL 26TH

Umareyn: That's the Way it Works

MAGIC: SACRED POOL
CONSTELLATION: WILDRONAE, CANES VENATICI
PLANETARY ASSOCIATION: ASTEROIDS
FAERIE ASSISTANTS: TSUL 'KALU

Umareyn instructs those in her realm to understand the secret forces that move the world and those in her care often become researchers in atomic science, the occult, or the paranormal or anything that requires a microscope or a telescope to investigate. As children these are the ones that incessantly ask you "why". They seek to know and understand all they encounter.

These elfin come to understand the seasons, and other cyclic movements of the Universe and thus are not surprised that there are periods and patterns of depression or inhibition in life but know as well that the chance to rise follows every fall although rising up requires an effort that falling does not.

APRIL 27TH

Silelyn: Skips Away

MAGIC: THE MAGIC MIRROR
CONSTELLATION: ELPAN, CAMELOPARDALIS
PLANETARY ASSOCIATION: NEPTUNE
FAERIE ASSISTANTS: GUNAAKADEIT

Silelyn teaches those in his care how to depart unfortunate circumstances or relationships without regrets. They come to know that a similar but better situation or person awaits them elsewhere and they need not feel like they have to compromise their needs or their principles or make do with what they have when it is clearly inadequate.

At the same time, these elfin learn to forgive, to forgo blame and regrets and simply accept that it was no one's fault that things didn't work out, it just wasn't the right situation.

WHAT ARE ELVES LIKE WHEN THEY ARE ALONE? THEMS'ELVES.

WHAT ARE ELVES LIKE WHEN THEY ARE TOGETHER? THEMS'ELVES.

April 28th
Palethyn: Protected by the Wild
MAGIC: HORN OF CALLING
CONSTELLATION: CONIHA, AQUILA
PLANETARY ASSOCIATION: URANUS
FAERIE ASSISTANTS: KUSHTAKA

These elfin become very comfortable being on the cutting edge of the world and society. They hunger for excitement and attract others of a similar nature. While most folks feel comfortable in their apartments or houses, these feel more at ease being out in Nature often doing things that are risky or daring. However, in time these elfin are likely to become the space travelers, adventurers and astronauts of the future.

The fae in this spirit's care develop the daring to take risks for gain or to change their lives, or sometimes just to make life more exciting. In this life, they are obtaining both the power of daring and the exciting aura that appeals to many others.

April 29th
Kynzarel: Learns Quickly
MAGIC: CAULDRON OF REBIRTH
CONSTELLATION: NESNOR, NORMA
PLANETARY ASSOCIATION: MERCURY
FAERIE ASSISTANTS: DEOHAKO

These fae are becoming quick learners and most of what they achieve in this lifetime is learning how to learn or how to embrace learning rather than resist it. Because of this they often find careers in intellectual fields although for some of these it is their first lifetime doing so.

Typically, the elfin under this spirit's guidance have been very feeling beings in previous lifetimes, which does not mean they no longer feel, but they are in the process of developing an appreciation for information, fact and logic as well and in this way are expanding their powers in the world. When they combine these powers by charging their ceremonies with deep feeling as well as esoteric understanding, they become powerful occultists indeed.

April 30th

Erynfel: Eager to Get Going

MAGIC: HORN OF CALLING
CONSTELLATION: LANU, ARA
PLANETARY ASSOCIATION: PLUTO
FAERIE ASSISTANTS: NIMERIGAR

Many of the elfin under this spirit's influence are so eager they are born prematurely. This Shining One teaches them how to develop patience without losing their ardor. These fae have heard the Call and they are ready, willing and eager to proceed.

These elfin are here to learn how to pursue their desires without being controlled by them. It is not about relinquishing their desires but mastering them. These fae come to understand that desires are spirits, powers and sometimes demons and as magicians it is their duty and right to direct and guide their desires to fulfillment in keeping with their Will and spiritual evolution.

THE SHINING ONES SAY WE SHOULD TRY TO MAKE EACH DAY A LITTLE BIT BRIGHTER.

> *We do not aspire to be Shining Ones, but to be our own true s'elves and on achieving that, we become ever more beings of light.*

> *The Universe is not a stagnant structure but a living being and thus we are wise to be ever adaptable in encountering it.*

> *Some think we elves are too gentle for this sometimes violent world. But we see it as a wild horse needing to be tamed.*

> *We elves do not look upon the Shining Ones as Gods or even as our bosses, but as those whose every act of being inspires us.*

MAY

HALYNFÈL: LINKS LIKE TO LIKE

MONTH: MAY

MAGIC: WITCHCRAFT

CONTINENT: SOUTHEAST ASIA, INDIA, TIBET, NEPAL AND BHUTAN

CONSTELLATION: ACANTHA, CIRCINUS

PLANETARY ASSOCIATION: ASTEROID BELT

FAERIE ASSISTANTS: GARUDA

This Shining One oversees those born or living in Southeast Asia, Tibet, India, Nepal and Bhutan. He is the patron of witches and teaches the art of witchcraft. He loves puzzles and thus guides puzzle makers, Sudoku players, detectives, maze builders, or simply those who feel stuck in life and are looking for a way out of some current predicament.

Beaal: Mystic Master
MAY 1ST TO 10TH
MAGIC: BON MAGIC
AREA: INDIA, TIBET, NEPAL, BHUTAN
CONSTELLATION: PUTOR, SCULPTOR
PLANETARY ASSOCIATION: ASTEROIDS
FAERIE ASSISTANTS: DAKINIS

This Shining One is a Master of Mysticism and is aided by the Dakinis, the higher spirits of India, Nepal, Tibet and Bhutan. He can teach the secrets of Trance states, how to enter into them, maintain them and what to do within these states. He also teaches those under his care how to take care of reptiles and how to integrate their influence into one's magic. He is a Visionary and thus can see possibilities far, far into the future. He can also inform the inquirer on how to be safe while astral traveling and how to confront and deal with demons/nightmares in lucid dreaming.

Redåndal: Master of Mudras
MAY 11TH TO 20TH
MAGIC: BUDDHIST MAGIC
AREA: SOUTHEAST ASIA
CONSTELLATION: ARAK, SAGITTARIUS
PLANETARY ASSOCIATION: ASTEROIDS
FAERIE ASSISTANTS: CHINTHE

Redåndal is the Master of Mudras or hand signs used in magic everywhere from Buddhist magic to Ninja magic. She can also teach one the various 'god-forms' or stances associated with magical ritual. The Chinthe, which are related to Griffins and which are temple or sanctuary guardians, assist her. Thus she can also teach the magician how to use mudras to instill protection over hir magical tools and implements. She knows great secrets concerning all these things that she will reveal to the worthy elfin magic worker including how to create magic swords, rings and other tools of power.

TO THE ELVES, CREATIVITY AND MAGIC ARE THE SAME.

Farynval: Uses What Works
MAY 21ST TO 31ST
MAGIC: HEDGEWITCHERY

AREA: PHILIPPINES

CONSTELLATION: ARAK, SAGITTARIUS

PLANETARY ASSOCIATION: URANUS

FAERIE ASSISTANTS: BAKUNAWA

Farynval is a very practical spirit and specializes in Hedgewitchery, or practical everyday magic. She is assisted by the Bakunawa or Sea Dragons. She teaches the magician how to make everyday chores into acts of magic so that the simplest task can prove beneficial in many ways. She can also reveal how daily routines can be magical rituals empowering one's life and spreading one's influence into the world. She is particularly a guardian of the wee folk, the little people, the brownies and others. She will further reveal to the elfin magician how small acts can accumulate into large powers and how productivity is more about doing a little regularly than a lot every once in awhile.

MAY 1ST
Wemerda: Walks in the Rain
MAGIC: THE MAGIC MIRROR

CONSTELLATION: PUTOR, SCULPTOR

PLANETARY ASSOCIATION: ASTEROIDS

FAERIE ASSISTANTS: WERE-BOAR

The elfin in this Shining One's care are either about to end a series of lifetimes and the lessons they need to learn within it or are beginning a new series of lessons and becoming acquainted with their new mission or assignment. They tend to have a sense that this life is of great import although they may not know exactly why this is so, merely that they could be called on at anytime to do something highly significant for the world or humanity.

In many ways, these fae are a reflection of a greater transition taking place in humanity and its evolutionary development overall and this is what gives them this sense of immensity of expectation. As their life proceeds, they come to gain more specific knowledge of their role in this transforming world and begin to do those things that destiny has assigned to them.

May 2ND

Uthynre: They Wait Patiently

Magic: Faery Circle

Constellation: Nesnor, Norma

Planetary Association: Sun

Faerie Assistants: Orang bunian

This spirit teaches those in her care to fit in nearly anywhere. These elfin become the reserve forces, so to speak, ready to fill in when and where needed. They bide their time but are ever ready to spring into action.

These are not on the back bench because they are the second string players, but are there because they are the elite corps called in when truly needed. These fae are becoming experts at what they do and thus only called when necessary and are otherwise free to pursue their own goals and ambitions in the meantime.

> *THE GREATEST AMBITION OF MOST ELVES IS TO LIVE TOGETHER IN LOVE, PEACE, AND HARMONY.*

May 3ʳᴰ

Mordåna: Mysteries Revealed

MAGIC: STAFF OF POWER
CONSTELLATION: ORMYN, CENTAURUS
PLANETARY ASSOCIATION: SATURN
FAERIE ASSISTANTS: BARONG

Mordåna is in charge of revealing specific mysteries to those under her influence according to the individual elfae's need and level of development. These revelations will increase their power and ability as elfin magician enchanters.

Naturally, these elfin are also those who are practicing, even playing with, these newfound powers, revelations and illuminations, becoming accustomed to wielding them so they become adept in their use so that the powers become second nature. Later, when they have truly mastered them, they will be shown what the true purpose is in having them.

May 4ᵀᴴ

Åbrele: A Life of Love

MAGIC: HORN OF CALLING
CONSTELLATION: PYKTAR, SAGITTA
PLANETARY ASSOCIATION: URANUS
FAERIE ASSISTANTS: KERE

This Shining One teaches the power of courtesy, how being obliging creates an atmosphere of success and respect.

However, these elfin can be somewhat flighty, resistant to making commitments in relationship, and ever seeking new relationships and new friends. This is particularly true as they master the art of courtesy and thus make friends and obtain lovers easily. The art of enchantment is usually their major field of study and they become ganconers or love talkers in time.

May 5th

Geåle: Now Everything Falls into Place

MAGIC: FAERY CIRCLE
CONSTELLATION: RAGOL, VIRGO
PLANETARY ASSOCIATION: URANUS
FAERIE ASSISTANTS: MAHA-PUDMA

Geåle gives those under his influence the sense that everything is coming together, that the Universe and the World is in fact working out just the way it should, despite all appearances to the contrary, and that everything happens for the best.

This is not an easy path for those just coming to it and the temptation to fall into depression or become prey to a negative outlook can be common until they truly master the lessons of this spirit. Once they do, they begin to perceive that their positive outlook as well as calm acceptance of those things that are currently beyond their personal power not only gives them a sense of peace but also subtly changes the world and especially their own lives for the better.

May 6th

Zolånfe: Would Like to Know the Truth

MAGIC: SACRED POOL
CONSTELLATION: GRADLI, TUCANA
PLANETARY ASSOCIATION: MOON
FAERIE ASSISTANTS: CHAKORA

These elves are struggling to understand the true nature of reality.

On the one hand, they want to believe and have faith, on the other they don't want to be ones who simply believe what they are told with absolutely no evidence to confirm their beliefs. Thus these often have a tendency to agnosticism, or a basic scientific approach to life, reserving their judgment about things until they have enough data to make a clear decision. Alas, they discover in time that there is never enough data, the data is always changing, what one thinks is true is often proven to be wrong later and that a provisional faith that helps one move forward but that can be altered as needed is the best solution to their dilemma.

May 7th
Feådera: Extremely Open
MAGIC: SHIELD OF LOVE AND PROTECTION
CONSTELLATION: FAERO, TRIANGULUM
PLANETARY ASSOCIATION: MERCURY
FAERIE ASSISTANTS: NĀGAS

Those that are influenced by being born under this spirit are taught to be open to all things, never to close their minds about anything, and always to be eager to learn and adjust their understanding. They are also shown that being respectful of other's opinions is the only way that one might influence them.

However, these elfin are usually more feeling than intellectual in nature and their openness is not just about ideas but an emotional willingness to embrace life and others. Those that are new to this course of development are sometimes unwilling to face reality, wish to hide from life and the world, feel that they have been hurt more than they can bear and just hide their feelings, but then that is exactly why they have been put under this Shining One's care and protection, who will help them open up and free thems'elves from the past.

May 8th

Ålålyndrys: Ahead of the Game

MAGIC: THE MAGIC MIRROR
CONSTELLATION: ATAROLD, MONOCEROS
PLANETARY ASSOCIATION: MERCURY
FAERIE ASSISTANTS: YAKSHA

The elfin born here are often ahead of the game, the heads of their class, although this can be because they are extremely sharp or because they are repeating a lesson that they've encountered previously and it is all becoming familiar and second nature to them.

Yet, either way, this Shining One will challenge these fae with events and developments that they did not consider possible making them scramble to keep up. In time, however, they will get the hang of it all and will turn the world on its head. Perhaps the lesson here is even when you are the best you should not make too many assumptions nor take things for granted.

May 9th

Paryndal: Psychic Premonitions

MAGIC: THE RINGS OF POWER
CONSTELLATION: HELON, SCUTUM
PLANETARY ASSOCIATION: MARS
FAERIE ASSISTANTS: KARAVIKA

This spirit instructs those who have come for his guidance how to have, and what to do with, premonitions and visions of the future. He also teaches that the future is a crossroads of tendency and possibility and that what one sees may not be what happens if one is wise enough to see it in time. One can change course or continue forward as deemed fit.

These fae often feel that they are overwhelmed by the impressions of the world and this spirit will aid them to attain an inner equilibrium that sustains them though their psychic episodes so they learn to be transpersonal in their visionary experiences, able to see what is coming without having their entire psyche thrown into disorder.

May 10th

Jyndarel: In the Right Direction

MAGIC: SHIELD OF LOVE AND PROTECTION
CONSTELLATION: PIHYR, SEXTANS
PLANETARY ASSOCIATION: URANUS
FAERIE ASSISTANTS: KINNARA

Those who come under this spirit's aegis are usually born here for a slight adjustment to their evolutionary course. This is not normally a large change but more of a tune up of their directional flow. For the most part, they have usually done quite well in previous lifetimes and need but make a small change or two to make them more effective and efficient as magicians.

These elfin develop transformative thinking and when they are nearing completion with this spirit come to be adept at helping others to improve thems'elves. They are the ultimate makeover artists.

> YOU COULD THINK OF THE SHINING ONES AS TEACHERS. BUT IF THEY TEACH, IT IS BY EXAMPLE ONLY.

May 11th

Zynfel: Yet to Come

MAGIC: HORN OF CALLING
CONSTELLATION: NERON, MENSA
PLANETARY ASSOCIATION: NEPTUNE
FAERIE ASSISTANTS: FLYING SERPENT

The elfin born here generally sense that there is something missing from thems'elves, some energy or power that has as yet not been achieved or granted to them and they seek their entire lives for the missing element or person. As they near the end of this spirit's course of study, they do indeed find what they are looking for, that which will move them powerfully forward in their evolution. This gives them a sense of renewal, a fresh start and a revitalized spirit and they proceed forward with optimism and a confidence that there truly is meaning and purpose to their lives.

May 12th

Doreryn: Courageously Goes On

MAGIC: THE RINGS OF POWER
CONSTELLATION: IRANALI, PICTOR
PLANETARY ASSOCIATION: EARTH
FAERIE ASSISTANTS: GARUNDA

Doreryn aids those who have suffered much to carry on despite all that they have endured. She demonstrates that life moves in cycles and that if you don't cling to the past that time and circumstances will provide one with new opportunities for a better life and an elevated position on the hierarchy of evolutionary development that brings with it the protection, power and privileges of those who have achieved.

The Shining Ones

These elfin are often very practical individuals who are learning to take one day at a time and to live in the now. Because of this simple and very real gravity as individuals, they come to be deeply respected and find that they can easily influence others.

MAY 13TH

Leånorfyn: Lives for the Future

MAGIC: THE STONE OF THE LAND
CONSTELLATION: MADON LUPRAE, CANIS MINOR
PLANETARY ASSOCIATION: NEPTUNE
FAERIE ASSISTANTS: YAKSHINIS

These elfin are visionaries who are ever creating with the future in mind. They see what can be and work to create it. This spirit teaches them how to enlist others to their cause and to share their vision in such a way that it enthuses willing helpers.

Sometimes these fae are perceived as message bringers. It is as though they are revealing a bit of the future to those who are ready; and indeed they are. These elfin become expert at establishing elven vortexes, witches' covens, sorcerers' parties, magicians' lodges or other organizations that can carry on the vision into the future.

MAY 14TH

Evyndreyn: Emotional Calm

MAGIC: CAULDRON OF REBIRTH
CONSTELLATION: GATH, CRUX
PLANETARY ASSOCIATION: PLUTO
FAERIE ASSISTANTS: TOYOL

Evyndreyn shows those elfin in her care how to calm their

emotions so they are no longer prone to stress related diseases or victims to sudden changes of circumstance. This does not mean they eliminate their feelings altogether and become unfeeling individuals or become totally unemotional, but rather they learn how to master their emotions and direct them toward the fulfillment of their will rather than having them as demons that kick them about from one day to another.

These become very vital individuals who instead of wasting their energy in tantrums and emotional trauma learn to keep their high level of energy going and can thus accomplish much that most others are too exhausted to even attempt. People often observe them and wonder, where do they get all the energy?

May 15th

Maråvyn: Mind Wielder

MAGIC: THE MAGIC MIRROR
CONSTELLATION: SALMO, PISCES AUSTRINUS
PLANETARY ASSOCIATION: URANUS
FAERIE ASSISTANTS: JARITA

These powerful magicians learn how to absorb energy from any environment and channel it toward the fulfillment of their vision. However, this spirit teaches them how to use this ability without becoming parasitic. These elfin don't merely take from the environment and those around them, but cycle the energy so that it flows through them and around again in a sort of energetic massage that enhances everyone. They become like an electro-magnet creating energy and power.

May 16th
Zänådor: With the Right People
MAGIC: SACRED POOL
CONSTELLATION: ÅNLEA, ANTLIA
PLANETARY ASSOCIATION: ASTEROIDS
FAERIE ASSISTANTS: PELESIT

Those born under the influence of this spirit are learning the lessons of right companionship. It is very important that they hang out with the right people for bad company will truly lead them astray.

Once they learn this lesson, they tend to have a very pleasurable and fulfilling life for they find those who not only help them to progress spiritually but who are stimulating, inspiring and a joy to be around. Life from then on is truly a celebration.

May 17th
Theyndre: Started A New Movement
MAGIC: SPEAR OF LIGHT AND DESTINY
CONSTELLATION: NERON, MENSA
PLANETARY ASSOCIATION: SUN
FAERIE ASSISTANTS: HANTU RAYA

Theyndre helps those in her care to start new movements. If you've ever wanted to get something new going in the world, you've been born in the right place.

While these tend to be very bold individuals, this Shining One teaches them how to understand others, how to speak and appeal to their needs and desires and how to arouse their interest and channel this energy toward the realization of a higher goal. These elfin come to know how to make others feel important and necessary to the fulfillment of the vision.

May 18th

Evardre: Elfin Ways

Magic: The Rings of Power
Constellation: Foli, Lyra
Planetary Association: Jupiter
Faerie Assistants: Nang Takian

This spirit teaches the philosophies and the special magic of Faerie. These magics work particularly well in the Faerie dimensions and thus they enable one to go into and out of Faerie with increasing ease.

These elfin learn to focus their energy and concentrate it toward the desired goal for these magics require a subtlety and maturity that is not always found in the average magician and is certainly not obtained by those who are dilettantes or mere dabblers.

May 19th

Gelynle: Followed By Magic

Magic: Cauldron of Abundance, Cornucopia
Constellation: Rochila, Pegasus
Planetary Association: Mercury
Faerie Assistants: Nariphon

Gelynle teaches the art of doing magic by being magic or the art of doing by non-doing. These fae develop to such a degree that they need do nothing more than be their own true s'elves and in response the environment and those around them are deeply affected.

The Shining Ones

Because of this power, these elfin are seen as being effortlessly persuasive and powerful without trying. They generally develop magnetic personalities, for people are naturally attracted to those who seem to be wise in ways they do not understand.

May 20th

Jiniryn: I Trust
Magic: Faery Circle
Constellation: Mefit, Cepheus
Planetary Association: Venus
Faerie Assistants: Singa

This Shining One trains those under him to trust, not simply have faith in the system, but to trust or learn to trust others as well as to recognize very quickly who is trustworthy. Naturally, some of those born in this spirit's care have trust issues, which is why this lesson is so important to them. They are here to learn that while not everyone is worthy of trust, perhaps even that most cannot be relied upon, that there are those one can trust if one can learn to recognize them.

As they advance in this teaching, these elfin learn how giving trust causes the recipient of that trust, to trust one in turn, and other secrets that lead to both leadership and success in magic.

To the elves, the future and the past are one. They each contain something wondrous to embrace.

MAY 21ST

Ilowyn: Healed Within

MAGIC: FAERY CIRCLE
CONSTELLATION: JANEL, GRUS
PLANETARY ASSOCIATION: MOON
FAERIE ASSISTANTS: MAYURA

This Shining One teaches the elfin under his leadership how to heal thems'elves internally. Often these fae study Reiki, Qigong, or other systems for internally channeling and moving energy. Naturally, when they fully master this technique they can use it to heal others, but this is especially the place of *healer, heal thys'elf*.

One of the first things they learn is how to trust what they feel, how to have confidence in their ability to truly focus and move the energy within their body and most of all to have enough confidence to do it and not be hampered by doubt. Those who are new to this often give up at first because their mind insistently questions whether such healing is even possible, however, if they persevere they will become great healers and energy movers.

MAY 22ND

Rafynthe: Rushes to Get it Done

MAGIC: THE STONE OF THE LAND
CONSTELLATION: WAND, MICROSCOPIUM
PLANETARY ASSOCIATION: VENUS
FAERIE ASSISTANTS: ABATH

The elfin born here have something they need to accomplish and Rafynthe is dedicated to helping them achieve this goal, whatever it may be. First, of course, they need to figure out exactly what it is they need to do and usually it is something they came near to completing in a previous lifetime but had not quite mastered. This is their time and if they devote thems'elves to it completely, they will surely find success with this Shining One's aid.

Thus these elfin often feel like there just isn't enough time. They were cut short in their former life and often fear that it will happen again. As they relax into their goal, however, they generally discover that they have been graced in this lifetime and will have all the time they need to complete this movement in their spiritual evolution.

May 23rd

Remervyn: Seeker of the Truth

MAGIC: FAERY CIRCLE
CONSTELLATION: FROHAMËL, COMA BERENICES
PLANETARY ASSOCIATION: URANUS
FAERIE ASSISTANTS: ASTOMI

This spirit helps those in her domain not only to seek the truth in the world but most of all to always embrace the truth about thems'elves, their situation and the challenges they face in order to become what they truly need and desire to be.

Often these elfin have some geas or obligation upon them that they must fulfill to go on. They are seldom eager to accept this fact but it is not until they do so that they can achieve this quest and in this way open the doorway to opportunity.

> *FROM THE ELVEN POINT OF VIEW, MANY FOLKS ARE SO DESPERATE FOR LOVE BECAUSE THEY ARE SO STINGY IN SHARING IT.*

May 24th

Treåvyn: Struck Gold

MAGIC: SACRED POOL
CONSTELLATION: MEFIT, CEPHEUS
PLANETARY ASSOCIATION: JUPITER
FAERIE ASSISTANTS: GAṆA

These elfin may feel like they have or will strike gold in life. They have a feeling that success is their destiny and they just need to keep searching and digging until they find it.

With the help of this spirit, these elfin become very practical in their approach to success, learning the fundamental skills that lead to success in the material world. They tend to enjoy and often attain luxury and as long as they don't fall prey to the demon of indolence all should go well for them.

May 25th

Zalåle: Wishfully Hoping

MAGIC: CAULDRON OF REBIRTH
CONSTELLATION: RIFRO, PHOENIX
PLANETARY ASSOCIATION: ASTEROIDS
FAERIE ASSISTANTS: GANDHARVA

It is true that the elfin born here are sometimes prone to wishful thinking, regardless of reality or any real prospect of the fulfillment of their fanciful wishes. On the other hand, they are here to learn to merge the two and will in time become powerful enchanters who fulfill the wishes of others. That is, after all, what elven magic is all about, making dreams and wishes come true.

In some cases, the opposite is true. Some born under the care of this spirit wouldn't know a fantasy or a wish if it bit them in their most fanciful place and are born here to learn to imagine and trust in the power of their imagination. They, too, will learn to make dreams come true.

May 26th

Wisaryl: Wanting to Help

MAGIC: THE STONE OF THE LAND
CONSTELLATION: ELFASA, DELPHINUS
PLANETARY ASSOCIATION: SUN
FAERIE ASSISTANTS: APSARA

Wisaryl aids those in his demesne to find appropriate service, for these elfin are usually willing servers but often don't know what precisely it is they can do that will truly be of help. To them it often seems that any effort is just a drop in the bucket compared to what needs to be done and Wisaryl aids them to find that service that will be truly fulfilling for them.

These elfin become radiant beings with an enormous will to live and great vitality. They are inspiring to others and in time become leaders in their field organizing others toward service as well. Often these find careers in Greenpeace, working with the poor or homeless or some other worthy cause.

May 27th

Sidare: Studies the Ancient Techniques

MAGIC: FAERY CIRCLE
CONSTELLATION: RAGOL, VIRGO
PLANETARY ASSOCIATION: SUN
FAERIE ASSISTANTS: VANADEVATAS

These fae frequently feel a calling to search for the most ancient techniques of magic and mysticism. They are not merely seeking generalized texts and philosophies but practical spells and techniques for achieving their goals. They believe deeply in the wisdom of the ancients and that there are lost or hidden formulas that if discovered will make them incredibly powerful.

These elfin also have a propensity for establishing thems'elves in traditional society for they often value history and tradition and can become very powerful ceremonial magicians. They will help establish elven homes and societies for the future.

May 28th

Jynvidral: Insightful Words

Magic: Cauldron of Rebirth
Constellation: Syrjae, Bootes
Planetary Association: Neptune
Faerie Assistants: Gramadevata

The elfin born under this spirit are here to learn how to say the right thing at the right time, thus they will become, through the course of their development if they pursue these lessons with earnestness, powerful public speakers or performers.

It is true that some who are just beginning under this spirit's instruction are shy, hesitant or uneasy about public appearance or speaking and thus this path requires tremendous tenacity, determination and hard work. The more advanced students are on the verge of becoming masters of public speaking with a powerful ability to influence others and will be able to sway large portions of the population at will.

May 29th

Arynde: Art of Wonder
MAGIC: THE STONE OF THE LAND
CONSTELLATION: JUFI, OCTANS
PLANETARY ASSOCIATION: SATURN
FAERIE ASSISTANTS: LOKAPALA

Arynde teaches the art of creating wonders, thus those under this spirit's supervision are often interested in movie making or in stage magic or illusion, as well as being truly great magicians of the spiritual or occult kind. They can also be interior decorators, set designers or have careers in anything where they create the wondrous.

These fae are often very open, even eager to receive inspiration and gain the technique of being inspired by everything and everyone. The world speaks to them of miracles and they translate this into life.

May 30th

Chilynde: Called by the Stars
MAGIC: HORN OF CALLING
CONSTELLATION: NALON, CORVUS
PLANETARY ASSOCIATION: MERCURY
FAERIE ASSISTANTS: HYANG

These elfin feel called to a higher destiny and under this spirit's guidance come to understand the evolutionary trend of their soulful spirit through lifetimes of development. While not all will or can be revealed to them in regard to this, they will surely learn much more than most understand.

However, because of this these elfin often feel trapped in the world as it is. They frequently cannot wait to be out of it and onto a higher dimension and more often than not feel like they just don't belong here. None-the-less, to move on they must come to terms with this plane of being and when they have mastered it will be launched into the higher dimension that they intuitively feel is their true home.

May 31ST

Felisa: Faery Bound
MAGIC: SPEAR OF LIGHT AND DESTINY
CONSTELLATION: FAERO, TRIANGULUM
PLANETARY ASSOCIATION: URANUS
FAERIE ASSISTANTS: APSARAS

These elfin are faerie bound and are determined to help this world fulfill its inner Faerie nature, so Faerie can manifest here on Earth. These elfin generally have very high ideals, sometimes too high, and can get in their own way by trying to achieve more than is reasonably possible at this time or can wait so long for the right one or moment to come along that they miss all the opportunities that do present themselves.

Felisa teaches them how to make the most of what they have, to use it to its fullness and to take the very smallest bit of magic or faery dust and get the greatest results from it. They are determined elfin but need to learn a little practicality.

IF YOU ARE LOOKING FOR THE KEYS TO THE HIGHER DIMENSIONS, THE SHINING ONES ARE THOSE KEYS.

JUNE

Niådyndėl: In the Great Circle
Month: June
Magic: Ceremonial Magic
Continent: Asia
Constellation: Ormyn, Centaurus
Planetary Association: Uranus
Faerie Assistants: Long Ma

Niådyndėl watches over those born in June and inspires those who do ritual or ceremonial magic. She is the guardian of those born in or who live in Asia, including Japan, but not the Philippines, which is under the influence of Southeast Asia. She is also the protector and guardian of prostitutes and sex workers of all kinds.

Orelynval: Attuned to Nature
JUNE 1ST TO 10TH
Magic: Taoist Magic
Area: China
Constellation: Larca, Leo
Planetary Association: Saturn
Faerie Assistants: Fenghuang

Orelynval, assisted by the Fenghuang that are related to the Phoenix, is the master of Taoist Magic. Her magic is the magic of wild places, particularly deserts, high mountains and other places that tend to be inhospitable to most men. She can teach one the Ways of Nature and how to lead a natural life away from the hustle and bustle of the World. She also reveals the underlying order of Nature and how to use this orderliness to achieve magical effects. She is associated with Saturn and thus appreciates dedication, earnestness and hard work.

Taråval: Guards the Sanctuaries
JUNE 11TH TO 20TH
MAGIC: SHINKYO
AREA: MONGOLIA AND KOREA, EASTERN RUSSIA
CONSTELLATION: ARAK, SAGITTARIUS
PLANETARY ASSOCIATION: JUPITER
FAERIE ASSISTANTS: HAETAE

This Shining One can aid one in understanding the ancient magic of Korea and associated areas. She is assisted by the Haetae that are dog/lion-like beings who are experts at pyromagery or the magic of fire, both using it for magic, relating to it and protecting ones'elf from it. Thus she is also associated with fire-walking. She teaches the mechanics of the Universe and how to deal with the elements and the elementals of the world. She also aids the elfin magician to see potential opportunity in every situation and how to turn any situation to one's positive advantage.

IF YOU LOOK THROUGH THE CORRIDORS OF TIME, YOU'LL FIND THE ELVES DANCING.

Ofinal: Touch of the Butterfly
JUNE 21ST TO 30TH
MAGIC: SHINTO MAGIC AND ONMYOJI

AREA: JAPAN

CONSTELLATION: OLÉLTRE, TELESCOPIUM

PLANETARY ASSOCIATION: PLUTO

FAERIE ASSISTANTS: BAKENEKO

Ofinal teaches Shinto Magic and Onmyoji. He is assisted by the Bakeneko, a supernatural cat being, and thus he teaches how to have magic familiars and how to make allies among animals that most folks only see as pets. He teaches the elf how to proceed fearlessly in life without being heedless of danger. He shows the elfin how to use meditation to achieve inner calm and how to use that calm to rise above everyday problems as well as to remain calm and steadfast in a crisis.

JUNE 1ST

Lodynfar: Loves to be Near You
MAGIC: STAFF OF POWER

CONSTELLATION: SYRJAE, BOOTES

PLANETARY ASSOCIATION: VENUS

FAERIE ASSISTANTS: AMABIE

Lodynfar teaches the underlying magic of relationship, friendship and association. He teaches one how to get close to people, how to give others the space they may need, and the cycles and rhythms of courtship.

Those who attain mastery of this spirit's instruction become very confident elfin enchanters and sorcerers who have a sense that they can go anywhere and make friends quickly and enlist these individuals' aid in their projects. These elfin also are more likely to get jobs easily and to be promoted more quickly.

June 2ⁿᵈ

Bearyn: Beautiful Evening
MAGIC: THE MAGIC MIRROR
CONSTELLATION: NERON, MENSA
PLANETARY ASSOCIATION: EARTH
FAERIE ASSISTANTS: BAKU

The elves under this spirit's guidance are here to learn the subtleties of social interaction, particularly the magic of the social gathering, the evening dinner, the cocktail party, etc. They are learning to schmooze. Those who are new to this spirit often find such interactions nearly unbearable; are frequently socially awkward; and hate such parties, but then that is why they are under this spirit's care.

Of course, this training isn't merely about group interaction, but also has a one-to-one element to it and the elfin training here learn the power of the intimate moment, the subtle magic of watching the moon together, the sunrise or the evening advancing.

June 3ʳᵈ

Lenåvyn: Looks Out from the Hiding Place
MAGIC: THE STONE OF THE LAND
CONSTELLATION: GRADLI, TUCANA
PLANETARY ASSOCIATION: ASTEROIDS
FAERIE ASSISTANTS: TANUKI

This spirit teaches those in his care how to hide their true s'elves even in the midst of a crowd. These elfin come to know how to protect their inner natures and preserve it in the face of those critical and sometimes callous individuals who scorn all that is different from them without giving in to such individuals or taking on their negative projections concerning one's nature.

Many elfin under this spirit's guidance are very sensitive individuals and what they are learning here is how to let the negative views of the world pass by without affecting them. They are gaining confidence in their own s'elves and their right to be who they truly are as well as determine their own direction in life without getting caught in the cycles of angry reaction that would keep them attached to those who belittle them.

JUNE 4TH

Imordyn: Healing Power of Love

MAGIC: THE MAGIC MIRROR
CONSTELLATION: FAERO, TRIANGULUM
PLANETARY ASSOCIATION: URANUS
FAERIE ASSISTANTS: KAPPA

Imordyn shows the elfin under her care that love truly heals if used correctly and without expectation of return. Imordyn will also reveal the underlying soulful nature of reality and how to tap into that energy to achieve whatever one desires.

These elfin also learn how to invest one's energy into those who are ready for it, for some individuals are simply not developed enough to appreciate the love they are given and thus will not be affected by it for lifetimes to come. Yet, true love seldom cares about such things, it loves because it needs to do so and trusts that while it may not have an immediate effect, that time will indeed heal all wounds.

June 5th

Lidynde: Loved by the Spirits

Magic: Faery Circle
Constellation: Tarle, Triangulum Australe
Planetary Association: Moon
Faerie Assistants: Peng

The elfin under Lidynde's influence have come to the attention of the supra-dimensional energies and are being especially guided and prepared for higher evolution. It is quite possible that the spirits in Lidynde's care have been the pets, dogs or cats, etc. and/or familiars of these higher spirits in aeons past and are still beloved to them.

These elfin are often quite direct beings, tend to be for the most part without guile and are ready to follow in the footsteps (?) flight-path (?) of their highly advanced mentors. Naturally, those who have been dogs and those who have been cats in previous lifetimes have a different approach to this movement of evolution.

June 6th

Vålalyn: Told the Time Has Come

Magic: Sacred Pool
Constellation: Prasugae, Lupus
Planetary Association: Mercury
Faerie Assistants: Bakeneko

These elfin have the feeling that something very important is about to occur and they can be called to serve and fulfill a mission at any time. This spirit helps them to be prepared for they indeed are *on call*.

These elfin are often living a life of grace as they await this call.

They are the recipients of a special dispensation and will find that they experience incredible luck as they await the moment when their talents and expertise or perhaps their sacrifice will be needed. This is, of course, a voluntary position.

JUNE 7TH

Vålyndyre: Touched by Wonder

MAGIC: HORN OF CALLING
CONSTELLATION: RYND, EQUULEUS
PLANETARY ASSOCIATION: PLUTO
FAERIE ASSISTANTS: DOKKAEBI

The elfin who receive the help of this spirit have or come to have encounters with the miraculous in their lives, which moves and touches them profoundly. Because of this they often have a strong sense of having guardian spirits or a personal guardian angel.

Sometimes, these experiences make them feel very apart from others around them who seem only interested in and only to experience mundane reality. Thus they often seek others like them or failing to find these develop more intimate relationships with the spirit world, although that tends to set them even further apart from normal humanity.

JUNE 8TH

Qidynde: Returns to the Beginning

MAGIC: FAERY CIRCLE
CONSTELLATION: ARANDUS, RETICULUM
PLANETARY ASSOCIATION: VENUS
FAERIE ASSISTANTS: WERE-FOX

Those who are born here are usually coming back to repeat lessons they have had before, often because they have decided that they want to fully master it before moving onward rather than having simply a cursory understanding of these life experiences. This is usually a voluntary act and not one that is forced upon them. They are determined to learn and master the fundamentals.

Sometimes, because of this, these individuals seem to be more stern or serious than most and others at times mistakenly think that they are repressed or have no feelings, but this is not the case, these elfin are deeply feeling individuals who will express thems'elves fully when the right moment or person comes.

June 9th

Uvalen: Things Move on their Own

Magic: Sacred Pool
Constellation: Ifol, Lynx
Planetary Association: Sun
Faerie Assistants: Ungnyeo

Uvalen teaches the elfin in her course of life study to see all the various magics and spells that affect the world and their situation and how these are all filtered and influenced by the laws and cycles of Nature and the Universe. She will further show them how magic, once released, like sound, will continue to move outward into space.

These elfin also come to see that less is more, that efficiency and technique is more powerful than brute force and even with small means one can achieve great things if their spell is done at the right time and place with true and sincere intention.

June 10th

Nidynve: Once Learned Always Remembered

MAGIC: SPEAR OF LIGHT AND DESTINY
CONSTELLATION: ALDAR, SERPENS
PLANETARY ASSOCIATION: VENUS
FAERIE ASSISTANTS: XIEZHI

Nidynve helps those under her influence to become memory masters, how to use memory houses, symbolic association and other techniques for calling information to mind easily. Thus these elfin come to be seen as incredibly knowledgeable individuals with great detail memory. Needless to say, once they begin mastering this course of study they do great in school and on tests and in time develop eidetic or photographic memory.

In terms of magic, these elfin can remember or recite spells without reference to any book, grimoire or text once they have learned it and thus they also frequently make good actors.

June 11th

Uvynre: Tiger at Heart

MAGIC: SHIELD OF LOVE AND PROTECTION
CONSTELLATION: EQALO, CETUS
PLANETARY ASSOCIATION: ASTEROIDS
FAERIE ASSISTANTS: YINGLONG

While these elfin may appear to be shy or withdrawn they are tigers at heart, particularly in defense of those they love or what they feel to be right and fair. If some villain mistakenly takes them on, such a miscreant will come to regret it deeply. These elfin cannot be bullied or pushed around. The wicked may beat them up but they will just keep coming back and the wicked will not escape without injury and will soon begin to sense there is easier prey elsewhere.

Thus these elfin are prone to be defenders of others who look to them for help, protection and guidance.

June 12th

Synmeryn: Songs of the Future

MAGIC: HORN OF CALLING
CONSTELLATION: TONENYS, PUPPIS
PLANETARY ASSOCIATION: SATURN
FAERIE ASSISTANTS: JIAOLONG

Nearly everything about the elfin who are born here calls out that here is someone who is ahead of hir time. Because of this these elfin often read or write science fiction and become visionaries of the future and all that it may bring. This Shining One helps these hone that precognitive ability.

These elves are most often very intelligent individuals with quick minds and keen insight. They usually love talking to others about what they see coming or about the ideas of the future they have encountered in the things they have read.

SOME FOLKS MISTAKE "SIMILARITY" FOR "SAMENESS". THE ELVES ARE ALL SIMILAR IN MANY WAYS, BUT NONE OF US ARE THE SAME.

June 13th

Vuarfyn: Untouched by the Madness of the World

MAGIC: THE MAGIC MIRROR
CONSTELLATION: FOCIDA, CHAMALEON
PLANETARY ASSOCIATION: MARS
FAERIE ASSISTANTS: BIXIE

Vuarfyn shows the elfin under her influence how to attain calm in a mad world and further how to take in the craziness of the world without being affected by it and to thus transform it into peace and quiet. No easy task this, and those new to this spirit often achieve calm only to be pulled away again and again and stirred up by the events in the world. In time, however, they learn to detach thems'elves from the woe is me, the end is coming madness that affects most modern media and to take it all with a shaker of salt. Thus they reflect back to the world something subtly different than that which world presented to them.

June 14th

Wulesyn: Watcher of the Wood

MAGIC: HORN OF CALLING
CONSTELLATION: FOLI, LYRA
PLANETARY ASSOCIATION: PLUTO
FAERIE ASSISTANTS: WINGED HORSE

Wulesyn teaches those who are born under her influence to become active observers. That is to say, they not only see but understand and are able to interpret what they see accurately, much on the order of Sherlock Holmes. Thus these individuals make great analysts for intelligence agencies, although they may be tempted to use these skills for gambling, at which they come to excel.

These are the sorcerers who become expert at identifying other individual's tells and can become experts at body language, neuro-linguistic programming or other disciplines that use these skills.

June 15th

Evilu: Elvish Charm

Magic: Cauldron of Rebirth
Constellation: Gath, Crux
Planetary Association: Sun
Faerie Assistants: Dilong

Evilu trains those in her care in the powers of charm and they will in time become very adept enchanters. She particularly shows these elfin how to empower others, especially those who have given up hope about themselves, with subtle charm and genuine flattery, that is to say by seeing their potential and praising it. Naturally, those who are helped by these elfin frequently come to be devoted to them and praise them highly in return.

Because of this power, people often refer to these elfin as being enlightening and as high spiritual beings. As long as they do not use this sense of evolved being as an excuse for separating thems'elves or raising thems'elves above others, all will go well.

> *We've heard men say they will hunt someone down to the ends of the Earth. Apparently they are unaware that it is round.*

June 16th

Lyndoreyn: Many Abilities

MAGIC: THE MAGIC MIRROR
CONSTELLATION: ARELO, AURIGA
PLANETARY ASSOCIATION: ASTEROIDS
FAERIE ASSISTANTS: TIANLONG

Elves in Lyndoreyn's care usually have multiple magical or psychic abilities that they are developing and she will aid them in coordinating these powers and using them to their fullest extent.

This life requires a lot of effort for the elfin born here and they frequently feel that they are under a great deal of pressure. Sometimes, particularly if they are just starting on this course of development, they feel at odds with thems'elves, as though they are emotionally or psychologically disjointed, or there is something missing from them, some key part that they need in order to really succeed. In time, this all clears up as their powers integrate into an effective and functioning whole.

June 17th

Zarvänse: Wolf-en Ways

MAGIC: THE RINGS OF POWER
CONSTELLATION: UNTWON, GEMINI
PLANETARY ASSOCIATION: SATURN
FAERIE ASSISTANTS: SHENLONG

This Shining One instructs those born in this place to reconnect or preserve the connection to their inner primal, animal s'elf without becoming overpowered or possessed by it, learning to let it flow forth when they are ready for it to do so.

These individuals often feel a great inner power surging through them. This is not only the power of their primal nature but also the more refined power of their will and the discipline they evoke to ride this power. They learn to ride the tiger or ride the dragon. Because of this they can become potent conjurors.

JUNE 18TH

Feordre: Faery Voice

MAGIC: CAULDRON OF ABUNDANCE, CORNUCOPIA
CONSTELLATION: JANEL, GRUS
PLANETARY ASSOCIATION: NEPTUNE
FAERIE ASSISTANTS: DRAGON TURTLE

Often these elfin are very quiet or shy until they speak or sing, then a great power, the vibration of Faerie issues from them amazing those around them. This Shining One helps them develop that power.

If they proceed with diligence they will be confident about their use of this power and will come to understand how it can be evoked not only to awaken the sense of Faerie in others, but will provide them with all they need to prosper in the world.

JUNE 19TH

Arove: Appears Ready

MAGIC: THE STONE OF THE LAND
CONSTELLATION: NESNOR, NORMA
PLANETARY ASSOCIATION: MERCURY
FAERIE ASSISTANTS: KARURA

This spirit instructs those born here in how to wait with confidence, how to obtain stability as a personality, and how to recognize the right time when it comes. The development of these qualities leads in time to greater responsibility and leadership.

Often those born here wonder if their chance will ever come. It seems they have been waiting all their lives for that moment and are eager to get started, get involved and get things going on a higher level. But, as we say, this spirit teaches calm patience and as these elfin learn this lesson they perceive that their powers are indeed still growing, that their time will come, and they need but wait and be ready.

JUNE 20TH

Bilefyn: Befriended by Elves

MAGIC: CAULDRON OF REBIRTH
CONSTELLATION: ORMYN, CENTAURUS
PLANETARY ASSOCIATION: PLUTO
FAERIE ASSISTANTS: SHŌJŌ

This spirit's influence aids one to open ones'elf to the vibration of Faerie, awaken to one's true Elfin nature and most of all to truly feel one's connection to the Spirit worlds and one's relations there.

It is true that these elfin often turn to the spirit world and their faerie kindred because they have come to sense that the normal world is an absolute desert for them with nothing to offer and no place for them to thrive. They may put on a brave face to the world but know that as it currently exists it is not the right place for them. Fortunately, their elfin kindred are looking out for them and will draw them ever closer to the Faerie realms.

> *MANY FOLKS FEEL GREED IS WHAT MOTIVATES THEM. THE ELVES KNOW IT IS WHAT ENSLAVES THEM.*

June 21ST

Volynde: Under the Stars
Magic: Staff of Power
Constellation: Jolor, Cygnus
Planetary Association: Jupiter
Faerie Assistants: Shang-Yang

While these elfin are clearly earth bound, they are beginning to become increasingly aware, under the influence of this Shining One, of their life among the stars and the destiny beyond earthly existence.

In many ways, these elfin are planting seeds that will bear fruit in far, far distant lifetimes in far, far distant space. They are enthusiastic about this, as most beginners tend to be and excited by the near infinite possibilities that lay before them. Yet, they must learn to live in the now as well and this spirit helps them effectively merge these two realizations. These elfin are learning to walk in starlight.

June 22ND

Tylynde: Hears Their Voices in the Rain
Magic: The Rings of Power
Constellation: Mefit, Cepheus
Planetary Association: Saturn
Faerie Assistants: Zhulong

Tylynde influences elfin who are developing psychic ability, particularly clairaudience and teaches those born here how to use water and/or feelings and emotions as channels for psychic perceptions. Thus those born here are prone to live near, or desire to live near rivers, lakes, or oceans. In lieu of this, they may have fountains, or running water sculptures in their homes or yards. Those that live with them may complain about a tendency some have to leave water running or dripping.

Because of their developing sensitivity, these elfin become attuned to the atmosphere of their environment and can use this power, if they desire or feel called to it, to attain fame and prestige.

June 23rd

Yndarth: Wildly Expressive

Magic: Sacred Pool
Constellation: Rochila, Pegasus
Planetary Association: Mars
Faerie Assistants: Tatsu

Yndarth influences those in his care to express thems'elves fully, to let their imaginations go free and to put it out there without forethought or artifice. Later, the lessons of refinement will be emphasized but that is the work of another spirit. Here, it is about getting it out, putting the first draft on paper, letting the ideas pour forth without filtering or critique and thus tapping into the great pool of possibility and inspiration.

These elfin are learning to express their creative being fully. They are like dancers, weight lifters, or other athletes who stretch before performing. First, they learn to loosen the muscles of the mind, later they apply discipline to the process.

> WHAT TRULY DEFINES THE ELVES IS OUR UNIQUE AND INDIVIDUAL BEINGS.

June 24th

Nådåde: Never Ceases to Strive

Magic: Horn of Calling
Constellation: Eqalo, Cetus
Planetary Association: Asteroids
Faerie Assistants: Uwan

These elfin are learning to never give up. They may pause, take a break, even retreat for a while, but the primary lesson of this spirit is to always come back again. This is the *when you fall off the horse you get right back on* school of evolutionary development.

Because of their own experience, these elfin can become adept at helping others to persevere. They make good counselors for alcoholics, smokers or drug addicts who are trying to give up their addictions or life counselors or couches in general. But their real calling is setting an example of spiritual devotion and progress on the path of s'elf realization.

June 25th

Meryntha: Moves in the Background

Magic: Spear of Light and Destiny
Constellation: Rochila, Pegasus
Planetary Association: Jupiter
Faerie Assistants: Yobuko

The elfin who are studying under this spirit are learning how to move powerfully behind the scenes, to affect things without seeking recognition, for they are learning that they are more effective and more powerful if their power goes unrecognized by all but the very few. These individuals often change the course of history but you will almost never find them mentioned in history books.

This power demands high intelligence as well as great maturity if it is to be used properly and not merely for personal advantage and profit. Thus these elfin are often developing both these qualities though this lifetime.

June 26th

Herynse: Peaceful Resolution

Magic: Faery Circle
Constellation: Fadon Luprae, Canis Major
Planetary Association: Mercury
Faerie Assistants: Yōsei

The elfin born here are learning the arts of arbitration and peacekeeping and thus make good marriage counselors as well are arbitrators in business or politics. They come to understand that fairness and justice, as well as equality for all concerned, are the only ways to create a permanent peace.

These elfin learn that tolerance, benevolence and kindness are key powers that aid them in their lives and their work. Alas, theirs is not an easy path particularly in a world where so many are eager to be in conflict with each other. In Elfin, these fae would be developing Warlocks or elfin who put a lock on or prevent war and conflict or arbitrate a just peace between warring parties.

> *In the end, we die as we were born and as we elves have ever lived, embracing the Mystery.*

June 27th

Refynve: Secret Understanding

Magic: Sacred Pool
Constellation: Math, Pyxis
Planetary Association: Asteroids
Faerie Assistants: Kijimuna

Refynve teaches esoteric secrets to those born here, each according to hir own level of magical maturity and evolutionary development. With this increased power these elfin can produce effects that seem truly magical and mysterious.

What these secrets are depend upon the individual and hir level of maturity, however, they each develop an aura of power and authority that is sensed by others who are in the least bit aware. People who encounter these elfin may feel that they are seeing the surface of an ocean but know that there is a vast depth unseen beneath that surface.

June 28th

Grånthor: Friendly Demeanor

Magic: Faery Circle
Constellation: Sarth, Vela
Planetary Association: Pluto
Faerie Assistants: Zashiki warashi

Grånthor instructs his elfin in the powers of friendliness and courtesy, networking, web-working, and the effectiveness of maintaining contact with one's friends, acquaintances and allies.

He also teaches them how positive contact with others, that is to say mutual and friendly interaction, is healing and beneficial to the wellbeing of each one and actually helps extend the lives of those involved. Thus these elfin are prone not only to live longer than normal folk but also to appear younger looking longer.

June 29th

Rådethe: Runs with the Pixies

MAGIC: HORN OF CALLING
CONSTELLATION: MEFIT, CEPHEUS
PLANETARY ASSOCIATION: MERCURY
FAERIE ASSISTANTS: ZUIJIN

These elfin are in this life to learn to let their hair down a bit, loosen that girdle, and let it all hang out, but not simply for their own sakes but in the pursuit of something higher. These are often somewhat hesitant or shy individuals, at least at the beginning, who are drawn out of their cocoon by a higher calling. They are not merely out to have fun, or have an adventure. Usually, their daring is only aroused by a call to justice or higher spiritual development. Faith makes them bold.

Those who are most advanced on this path begin to combine the personal with the spiritual and are often travelers, loving to explore new places and encounter new cultures and especially to meet others of their nature in their journeys.

June 30th

Hysynre: Guided by the Fireflies

MAGIC: SWORD OF TRUTH AND JUSTICE
CONSTELLATION: JANEL, GRUS
PLANETARY ASSOCIATION: URANUS
FAERIE ASSISTANTS: AMEONNA

Those under the guidance of this spirit are developing connections to the Faerie realms, particularly that of the faery folk who appear as dragonflies, butterflies, moths and fireflies. Most people think of these as mere insects, but these elfin come to understand the otherworldly nature of the insect realm and how to relate, communicate and use their association for magical power and effect. Think of Gandalf talking to the butterfly in the Lord of the Rings.

These elfin increasingly come to understand that all of Nature is alive and that all of the Universe is connected by magic and they are learning to make allies in this very important realm of Faerie being.

> *THE SHINING ONES ARE EAGER TO AID AND ASSIST US, BUT THEY WILL NEVER HELP US TO DO THOSE THINGS THAT DO NOT ULTIMATELY BENEFIT OUR SPIRITUAL AND EVOLUTIONARY DEVELOPMENT.*

> *IF YOU ASK THE ELVES WHAT THEY CELEBRATE, THEY WILL LIKELY REPLY, "NEARLY EVERYTHING".*

JULY

Rafièl: Weaving Spells
Month: July
Magic: Spellcraft
Continent: Australia, New Zealand and Micronesia
Constellation: Arandus, Reticulum
Planetary Association: Neptune
Faerie Assistants: Wati-kutjara

Rafièl oversees those born in July, teaches basic Spell Craft and guides those who live in or were born in Australia, New Zealand and Micronesia. His higher connection comes through the Constellation Reticulum that we elves call Arandus. He is the patron of ancient buildings, particularly the ruins of ancient civilizations and thus has great potency around ruined temples, ancient pyramids and even very old buildings.

Gylial: Blends With The Brush
JULY 1ST TO 10TH
Magic: Bush Magic
Area: Australia
Constellation: Rifro, Phoenix
Planetary Association: Venus
Faerie Assistants: Rainbow Serpent

Gylial is a master of Bush Magic, the magic of the outback and the wilds, particularly in the development of one's relationship to the Dreamtime, the world that is closer to Faerie than the more structured reality of normal consciousness. He also can help the magician find or connect to abandoned places or magics long forgotten and how to revitalize these spots or the magical vibration that still resides there. He is assisted by the Rainbow Serpents who are the masters of relating to parallel worlds. He is an inspiration to Dream Walkers.

Perynal: Among the Stones
JULY 11TH TO 20TH

MAGIC: MAORI MAGIC

AREA: NEW ZEALAND

CONSTELLATION: FADON LUPRAE, CANIS MAJOR

PLANETARY ASSOCIATION: MARS

FAERIE ASSISTANTS: PATUPAIREHE

This Shining One is assisted by the fairy elfin like Patupairehe and can teach one the ancient magics of the Maori people. She is adept at astral travel and can aid the elf in anything that involves moving out of hir body and exploring other worlds or dimensions, particularly the realms of the elementals, the fire, water, earth and air spirits and evoking those powers in one's magic.

> *IN A WORLD WHERE EVERY MAN IS FOR HIMSELF, THE ELVES ARE FOR EACH OTHER AND EVERYONE ELSE.*

Deånadål: Surfs the Sea
JULY 21ST TO 31ST
MAGIC: SEA MAGIC
AREA: MICRONESIA
CONSTELLATION: VÅSTARUVA, ANDROMEDA
PLANETARY ASSOCIATION: ASTEROIDS
FAERIE ASSISTANTS: ABAIA

Deånadål is the protector and instructor of children and young magicians and is assisted in this by the Abaia who are large mystical eel beings. She teaches those who approach her Sea Magic in its various forms and all things related to the magic of the waters. She will also instruct the elf on how to express hir spirit and how to be an individual without drawing the ire of the normal folk, the conforming mass, or how to survive and even prosper in an alien environment.

JULY 1ST

Shynthel: Sister of Our Hearts
MAGIC: THE RINGS OF POWER
CONSTELLATION: RYSTATA, CAELUM
PLANETARY ASSOCIATION: ASTEROIDS
FAERIE ASSISTANTS: BOBBI-BOBBI

This spirit instructs the elfin born here in the power of friendship. Those who are deflated when someone they desire responds to their approach with, "Can't we just be friends?" can learn much from this spirit who will teach them how being friends is the key and path to all that they desire.

Beginners on this path of magical instruction can take this seeming rejection rather hard, feeling their whole world has collapsed and embracing the offered friendship seems both a let down and the last thing they really wish to do; however, this Shining One will reveal that the opposite it true and that by being a true friend and a friend truly incredible opportunities will open for these elfin.

July 2ND

Ryndarvyn: Serves the Poor

MAGIC: THE STONE OF THE LAND
CONSTELLATION: EQALO, CETUS
PLANETARY ASSOCIATION: NEPTUNE
FAERIE ASSISTANTS: TANIWHA

These elfin are destined to be rulers and leaders for they are learning to take care of everyone in their realm of influence, to neglect none and to see to the needs of all, by which they encourage the land to prosper.

Sometimes, particularly for those who are just beginning this course of study, the elfin born here are endeavoring to make up for bad karma or ill deeds of the past, attempting to wash away the errors and regrets of their early life and earlier lifetimes. As they advance, however, these elfin come to understand that this is the path to peace and success in the world and their actions help bring the world into harmony.

July 3RD

Evifor: Elvish Ways

MAGIC: THE STONE OF THE LAND
CONSTELLATION: SALMO, PISCES AUSTRINUS
PLANETARY ASSOCIATION: MERCURY
FAERIE ASSISTANTS: KAITIAKI

This spirit inspires the elfin born here in the styles and the culture of Faerie and how the ancient forms and traditions of Faerie life can be integrated into the modern world or the particular ethnic culture they find thems'elves within.

These elfin become transformers, both of ancient elven culture and of modern culture, remaking the old and giving it rebirth in a fresh and vibrant form. They are in the process of developing great channeling ability, not so much of information, but of pure power applied to the world and its forms.

JULY 4TH
Årefyn: Amused by it All

MAGIC: CAULDRON OF ABUNDANCE, CORNUCOPIA
CONSTELLATION: EQALO, CETUS
PLANETARY ASSOCIATION: VENUS
FAERIE ASSISTANTS: TAOTAO MO'NA

Årefyn shows those in his care how to take the world and its folly with a grain of salt without becoming either callous or cruel in doing so. These elfin come to see the humor in life and their developing good natured approach to life brings them success and abundance. Of course, for elfin who have an aspiration in this direction, this is a great place for those who wish a career in comedy, satire, and so on.

While these elfin tend to see the wry side of life, they are also in the process of learning compassion in doing so. They have learned or are learning to forgive and this frees them considerably.

> *THE SOURCE OF ALL THINGS IS LOVE. WHEREVER YOU FIND LOVE, THERE YOU WILL FIND THE MAGIC BEING BORN.*

July 5th

Farynse: It is Always a Good Thing

MAGIC: FAERY CIRCLE
CONSTELLATION: NESNOR, NORMA
PLANETARY ASSOCIATION: NEPTUNE
FAERIE ASSISTANTS: TAPAIRU

This Shining One teaches those under her care to embrace the positive in every situation and circumstance, literally to see the light that is often the light at the end of the tunnel. These elfin are also learning to rely on the power of association and contact, the great power of having magical allies.

Because they develop the ability to see the positive, they are quick to notice opportunities, solutions and the easiest way forward and thus are prone to become great successes in the world.

July 6th

Rasudyn: Awakens the Magic

MAGIC: HORN OF CALLING
CONSTELLATION: KOFI, COLUMBA
PLANETARY ASSOCIATION: MARS
FAERIE ASSISTANTS: TIPUA

As these elfin develop, they obtain the power to transmit the vibrational energy of Faerie to others, awakening them not just intellectually but arousing their psyches in a deep and powerful way. Those who encounter them cannot help but feel there is something different and special about them.

Naturally, these elfin come to be powerful figures and thus they must resist the temptation to use this power for s'elf aggrandizement and personal success without consideration of others needs or development. The adepts of this school can easily become cult leaders or fall into the sway of the masses overwhelmed by their need for appreciation and popularity.

July 7th

Dongaryn: Could Be the Beginning of Something Wonderful

MAGIC: SACRED POOL

CONSTELLATION: RYSTATA, CAELUM

PLANETARY ASSOCIATION: MERCURY

FAERIE ASSISTANTS: BOLONG

Those who encounter these elfin in their adept stages of being are likely to feel that something marvelous is about to occur in their lives, for these elfin learn to arouse the possible and the fantastic in the hearts and minds of those they encounter. Often those who encounter them feel that, at last, life is going to be as they always imagined it would be.

At the same time, these elfin are taught that dangling carrots is not enough; one must also deliver a practical and stable path to follow for those who come to them. This place bears great responsibility for one will be given much and needs to use it wisely for the benefit of all.

> *What is an elf's duty? It is to become the best one can be and to help others do the same.*

July 8th

Lyndyndyn: Many Ways to Go

MAGIC: SHIELD OF LOVE AND PROTECTION
CONSTELLATION: ECH, HERCULES
PLANETARY ASSOCIATION: JUPITER
FAERIE ASSISTANTS: UNGUR

Those born here have come to a place of choice. They have freed thems'elves or are freeing thems'elves of karma that has bound them in the past and now are free to choose a new direction for their spiritual development. As this spirit reveals, which way they choose to pursue is entirely up to them and as long as they choose from their heart, that is as long as they are true to their own nature, they cannot make a mistake.

There is a certain amount of protection that comes with this place. They may, in the beginning, still feel uncertain due to the karma that they had to clear in previous lifetimes, but in this life they are being given a certain amount of freedom, a space in which to make a free choice without feeling compelled to go this way or that against their will.

July 9th

Luarve: Pixie Magic

MAGIC: SWORD OF TRUTH AND JUSTICE
CONSTELLATION: LOWA, ERIDANUS
PLANETARY ASSOCIATION: MERCURY
FAERIE ASSISTANTS: PATUPAIAREHE

Luarve teaches those under her influence about the higher laws of manifestation and how one may, without accumulating bad karma, transcend the mundane laws of man if one is indeed acting with these higher laws in mind. This is not an easy path, for discerning what is genuinely for the best of all concerned and separating it from the urge to just do what one wants regardless of others, can be a subtle and tricky thing to determine.

Thus these elfin often seek the association and guidance of those that they trust and that they see as role models of the higher spiritual principles and they in time become such role models as they develop adeptship in this area.

July 10th

Frenava: Feels the Possibilities

MAGIC: SHIELD OF LOVE AND PROTECTION
CONSTELLATION: NERON, MENSA
PLANETARY ASSOCIATION: SATURN
FAERIE ASSISTANTS: KELERU

The elfin in this Shining One's care develop an instinctive sense for opportunities. This is certainly a psychic power or sixth sense for recognizing possibilities for advancement, investment, or recognizing those who will respond in a positive way to the elfin's approach. Thus these fae develop a profound ability to succeed in the world.

These elfin, however, must be careful of making changes haphazardly. Because opportunities come so easily for them, they are prone in the beginning to seize each one that appears and make a change with no clear long-term plan or direction. This, of course, clears up as they become more and more adept and have a more precise knowledge of where they wish to go and how to get there.

> *THE WAY IS INDIVIDUAL BUT ALWAYS CONSIDERS WHAT IS FAIR FOR EVERYONE.*

July 11th

Evålese: Blessed by Moonlight
MAGIC: FAERY CIRCLE
CONSTELLATION: UNTWON, GEMINI
PLANETARY ASSOCIATION: MOON
FAERIE ASSISTANTS: JARAPIRI

These elfin are learning the power of the psyche and are often inclined to be night people who love the dark and adore the moonlight. Because of this there is often a moon-like glow to them or roundness to their faces.

Because of their moon association, these can be moody individuals at first, even manic-depressive until they learn to use the cycles of the moon to their benefit and adapt their personal energy to its fluctuations. This is also a lifetime when they are freeing thems'elves of emotional habits and traumas of the past and learning to forgive others and thems'elves. Of course, being moon people they can develop great cunning and the ability to act in secret or behind the scenes.

July 12th

Idyndre: Have Always Been a Feeler
MAGIC: SWORD OF TRUTH AND JUSTICE
CONSTELLATION: LANU, ARA
PLANETARY ASSOCIATION: VENUS
FAERIE ASSISTANTS: DIRAWONG

This Shining One teaches the power of feeling, or trusting one's feelings, particularly about what is right and fair. These become very powerful and determined elfin.

These elfin become very clear about what they feel, overcome all emotional confusion and use the power of their feelings and emotions to achieve what they will in the world. They are strong characters and when adept are not afraid to express their feelings and, in fact, are determined to do so.

JULY 13TH

Milelyn: Mutual Respect

MAGIC: THE STONE OF THE LAND
CONSTELLATION: ECH, HERCULES
PLANETARY ASSOCIATION: SATURN
FAERIE ASSISTANTS: DHAKHAN

This spirit teaches the fundamental and essential powers of fairness, justice and most of all mutual respect. The necessity of these powers in order to establish a stable world cannot be overestimated.

Once these elfin have evolved these powers sufficiently they can go nearly anywhere and are welcomed. They make great judges or arbitrators and when adept are absolutely trustworthy. Needless to say, many of those in this course of evolutionary study have been abused or have been abusers or both in previous lifetimes and have come to deeply understand the vital need for respect and fairness in the world.

> ONE MIGHT ASK IF THE ELVES ARE SUCH UNIQUE INDIVIDUALS HOW CAN THEY TRAVEL THE WAY TOGETHER. AND THE ANSWER IS, "QUITE EASILY!"

July 14th

Feleda: Driven by a Hunger to Excel

Magic: Sacred Pool
Constellation: Jufi, Octans
Planetary Association: Sun
Faerie Assistants: Hākuturi

Feleda aids those who are perfecting their s'elves and who wish to be the best at what they do. She teaches them how to achieve this exulted state without interfering with or envying others. These elves are essentially competing with thems'elves, ever striving to improve their performance.

Of course, being perfectionists, they often drive those around them crazy with their obsessive compulsive behaviors and this Shining One helps them to strive toward being greater without making too many demands on those around them.

July 15th

Elisyn: Dragon's Scales

Magic: Spear of Light and Destiny
Constellation: Foli, Lyra
Planetary Association: Mercury
Faerie Assistants: Krantjitinja

Elisyn helps the elfin in her sphere of influence to become tough individuals, especially to be psychically impermeable to astral assault or negative vibrations. These elfin learn to be utterly fearless. They evolve into individuals who are persistent, will never give up or back down when they are pursuing what is right. As adepts they don't even fear death, knowing that death is but a transition from one form to another.

These elfin give courage and hope to those around them who are amazed at their seeming indefatigability and their valiant nature that seems heedless of nearly all danger.

July 16th

Nifynsa: One Day It All Began to Make Sense

MAGIC: THE MAGIC MIRROR
CONSTELLATION: RALTOSOR, CORONA AUSTRALIS
PLANETARY ASSOCIATION: JUPITER
FAERIE ASSISTANTS: MAREIKURA

The elfin born here are beginning to comprehend the deeper secrets and mysteries of the Universe. This opens new worlds to them and they begin to see this world in a new way.

With this understanding comes greater powers and there is naturally a temptation to use this power strictly for personal gain and profit, which would accumulate karma that would end up binding them for numerous lifetimes, thus the significance of maturity is emphasized here.

July 17th

Avåndse: At Home Among the Elves

MAGIC: CAULDRON OF ABUNDANCE, CORNUCOPIA
CONSTELLATION: RYNGYL, APUS
PLANETARY ASSOCIATION: NEPTUNE
FAERIE ASSISTANTS: MIMIS

Those born here are developing the ability to fit into an elfin community easily, enjoying and bringing success and abundance to it. They have worked out many of the personal issues that prevent so many from living in community successfully.

They tend to be popular individuals but are also very practical, seeing what is needed in community and doing their best to provide it. Thus they are welcomed nearly everywhere. Their magic is enchantment but an enchantment that is both subtle (nearly invisible but no less powerful for being so) and group oriented.

JULY 18TH

Avare: At One with My Destiny

MAGIC: THE STONE OF THE LAND
CONSTELLATION: DEOSA, CANCER
PLANETARY ASSOCIATION: SUN
FAERIE ASSISTANTS: EMU

Avare helps those in his care to see, understand and accept their destiny and all that this entails for them. Many individuals feel in their hearts that they have a great destiny but the fae born here clearly come to understand all that it takes to fulfill their particular quest.

The acceptance of this fate gives these elfin great personal power and they are often seen as being strong minded. In the course of their evolution, all extraneous activities and effort is let go and they pursue their course with energy and determination and will not resist nor be repulsed from those things they know need to be done.

THE SHINING ONES ARE MORE VARIED THAN THE TREES AND MORE POPULOUS THAN THE STARS.

July 19th

Vålelynde: Took Great Will Power

MAGIC: THE RINGS OF POWER
CONSTELLATION: CONIHA, AQUILA
PLANETARY ASSOCIATION: SUN
FAERIE ASSISTANTS: LANGAL

This spirit helps develop will power in those who are under her influence so that it is a powerful tool for achieving whatever they need or desire. They are especially shown the need for discrimination, that is using their energy wisely and not wasting it on things that are ultimately insignificant. She also reveals the importance of right association and the need to find those who empower one on the path and to avoid those who merely waste one's time or that will lead one astray.

July 20th

Refyndys: Secret Knowledge

MAGIC: SHIELD OF LOVE AND PROTECTION
CONSTELLATION: URODELA, LACERTA
PLANETARY ASSOCIATION: JUPITER
FAERIE ASSISTANTS: WOINUNGGUR

Refyndys not only reveals many occult and esoteric secrets to those under his aegis, but he also trains these elfin how to protect that knowledge from those who are not ready for it. These elfin are slated, at least for a time, to be protectors of the inner secrets. It is their duty to carry this knowledge into the future revealing only to those that are truly worthy.

Those who are in the very early stages of this training often wish to run around shouting their secret knowledge to the rooftops as a means of s'elf validation; however, they soon learn the folly of doing so and come to understand that in this instance, secrecy preserves the wisdom they protect.

July 21ˢᵀ

Jolale: If the Time Comes

MAGIC: THE MAGIC MIRROR
CONSTELLATION: MADON LUPRAE, CANIS MINOR
PLANETARY ASSOCIATION: MERCURY
FAERIE ASSISTANTS: URE

These elfin are on hold in this lifetime, prepared and waiting for the right time to come when they will be needed and called upon. In the meantime, these individuals are relatively free to enjoy thems'elves and pursue their personal interests. This gives these elfin a sense of grace in this life, yet at the same time they inwardly know that at any point they could be called on a mission for the Shining Ones. Often what these elfin fear the most is that the *call* may never come.

July 22ᴺᴰ

Gydaryn: From the Distant Shores

MAGIC: SACRED POOL
CONSTELLATION: ÅNLEA, ANTLIA
PLANETARY ASSOCIATION: PLUTO
FAERIE ASSISTANTS: WANDIJANS

This Shining One is in charge of walk-ins, which is to say spirits from other planetary systems and dimensions who come here for a certain evolutionary lessons that are currently unavailable in their system. Naturally, they often feel displaced at first and frequently speak of not being human even though they do have human bodies.

Alas, these elfin often feel a sense of being limited or trapped at first, but as they become increasingly aware of their situation and the positive benefits of what they are learning here they also become accustomed to this alien environment and are able to fit in more easily.

JULY 23ʳᴅ

Hidale: Good Mother

MAGIC: FAERY CIRCLE
CONSTELLATION: LARCA, LEO
PLANETARY ASSOCIATION: MOON
FAERIE ASSISTANTS: GAMBIER

Hidale teaches the power of nurturing and those under her influence become great parents, teachers and couches. At the same time, these elfin have reached the end of a cycle of development and are being moved up to realms where they have greater power and responsibility.

This lifetime shows these individuals developing a degree of Transpersonality, of nurturing without judging, aiding each and everyone who comes to them to improve thems'elves and their lives.

FAERIES, PIXIES, BROWNIES, AND GNOMES ALL ARE WELCOME IN AN ELVEN HOME.

July 24th

Maråfyn: Message from the Stars

MAGIC: THE RINGS OF POWER
CONSTELLATION: DRAKAN, DRACO
PLANETARY ASSOCIATION: VENUS
FAERIE ASSISTANTS: YULU YULARA

The elfin under this Shining One's influence are in the process of becoming messengers for the Higher Powers; however, the messages they bring are not in the form of words usually, but gifts of energy and power. Those that come into contact with these fae are empowered by them, especially in an emotional or psychological way.

Curiously, they are not always aware or conscious of the gifts they bear or the missions they fulfill. They simply show up when needed, guided there instinctually and do what needs to be done at the time. Thus this life shows them gaining an increasing attunement to their instinctual awareness.

July 25th

Holedyn: Great Affection

MAGIC: SHIELD OF LOVE AND PROTECTION
CONSTELLATION: KAVA, SCORPIUS
PLANETARY ASSOCIATION: URANUS
FAERIE ASSISTANTS: MUIT

The elfin under this spirit's influence are learning to let thems'elves be guided by natural inclination and affection. They instinctually feel protective of certain individuals and this increases as they mature. They often adopt others in a spiritual sense, calling them their sons or daughters even when these individuals are not orphans and have natural parents. They are learning to be guides in this life and will increasingly assume that role with greater power in future lifetimes taking on the same job as this spirit who protects them, as this spirit evolves to greater things.

July 26th

Efynthe: Don't Suggest that Course of Action

Magic: Sacred Pool
Constellation: Drakan, Draco
Planetary Association: Uranus
Faerie Assistants: Munga Munga

Efynthe deals with elfin who have come to a dead-end in their progress, have taken a wrong turn, or have completed a course of study but are confused about what direction they should go in next. In this life, they are in a bit of a holding pattern while they catch their breath, so to speak, and have time to really consider their options. Often they have been working and struggling toward their goals so furiously that they failed to see they were painting thems'elves into a corner and now need to let the paint dry before they proceed onward.

Because of this they often feel they are subject to a cruel fate and living a life that makes no sense to them, but as they evolve in this life and learn patience an opportunity will come to them, usually out of the blue, that will provide a whole new revelation and direction for them.

> *At some point, our inner radiance penetrates all the cells of our being and we are transformed.*

July 27th

Evorådyl: Absolute Mastery

MAGIC: STAFF OF POWER
CONSTELLATION: WONSA, CASSIOPEIA
PLANETARY ASSOCIATION: JUPITER
FAERIE ASSISTANTS: NGALBJOD

The elfin born here are on the point of become true masters of the powers they have developed thus far through the lifetimes and because of this are often envied by those around them who mistakenly think that this is an accident of birth rather than the lifetimes of effort it truly represents.

It is very important that these individuals learn to empower others for otherwise their life will be marked by secret interference by the envious and endless and unnecessary competition. Still, they often feel they have been blessed in this life and that is surely true although this blessing comes primarily because of their own hard work.

July 28th

Åthyndrys: As Soon as Possible

MAGIC: SWORD OF TRUTH AND JUSTICE
CONSTELLATION: ULOS, TAURUS
PLANETARY ASSOCIATION: PLUTO
FAERIE ASSISTANTS: TANGATA

The elfin born here often cannot help but feel things are just not happening or evolving fast enough. They have seen the future, they know what is inevitably coming and what will make the world a better place and are eager to see that happen as well as frustrated that there are so many who don't comprehend what they tell them and others who just plain won't listen to the truth.

These elfin become strong independent beings, who are frequently inclined toward revolutionary views since they wish to restructure the world, want justice where it is lacking, and feel that things are just not developing quickly enough. They want it now and they just don't see why it shouldn't be so. It is what is right and fair after all and to the ultimate benefit of everyone.

JULY 29TH

Uvaråsys: Thinks it Through

MAGIC: THE STONE OF THE LAND
CONSTELLATION: VERPA, HYDRA
PLANETARY ASSOCIATION: MOON
FAERIE ASSISTANTS: KORAKORAKO

This Shining One instructs these elfin in the power of thoroughness and planning. This can be frustrating at first, particularly to those who are new to this training and who have a basic extraverted tendency to simply do and then deal with the consequences later. In this lifetime, they are learning that planning ahead can lead to fewer difficulties and fewer problems later; it is more efficient and demands less time and energy in the long run.

These individuals are on the path to becoming planners: architects, city planners, designers and in the course of time planners of space colonies or other systems. As fiction writers they tend to create entire worlds for their characters.

> TO THE ELVES, PARADISE AND ELFLAND AND HOME ALL MEAN THE SAME THING.

July 30th

Åvyndyl: Awaits the Opportunity

MAGIC: SPEAR OF LIGHT AND DESTINY
CONSTELLATION: ARANDUS, RETICULUM
PLANETARY ASSOCIATION: JUPITER
FAERIE ASSISTANTS: HEKETORO

This is group of elfin who are learning, under this spirit's instruction, how to wait for the right moment, how to apply force precisely so it will have maximum effect.

Once they have learned this lesson they can become very successful individuals in the material world or any world they choose to function within. To others they may appear to be very lucky or blessed, and in a sense they are, but really they are merely becoming very good at using their powers well.

July 31st

Reyndyn: Sees What Will Come Next

MAGIC: CAULDRON OF ABUNDANCE, CORNUCOPIA
CONSTELLATION: VERPA, HYDRA
PLANETARY ASSOCIATION: SUN
FAERIE ASSISTANTS: TUTUMAIAO

Reyndyn instructs the elfin born here in how to use precognitive abilities to gauge the movements and trends of societies. One can, of course, become quite rich by doing this. They are also able to alter or guide the flow of public opinion with this power.

Naturally, these elfin develop the power of attraction. They learn what to say or do to influence and affect everyone they encounter and thus are on the path to being powerful sorcerers.

AUGUST

Quarânèl: Makes Suggestions
Month: August
Magic: Sorcery
Continent: South America
Constellation: Holvoro, Fornax
Planetary Association: Mercury
Faerie Assistants: Spirits of Carnivale

This Spirit has his greatest influence in South America and over those who live or were born there. He is the Master Benefactor of all Sorcerers and is the patron of all illuminating plants and trees, and all entheogenic substances and those under their influence. He is also the guardian of lucid dreamers in the dream state and all entheobotanists.

Gyndåfal: Dances Down the Magic
AUGUST 1ST TO 10TH
Magic: Umbanda and Candomblé
Area: Brazil
Constellation: Elfasa, Delphinus
Planetary Association: Earth
Faerie Assistants: Saci

Gyndåfal, aided by Saci, the pixie like spirit of Brazil and his cousins, can inform the elf about the magic of Umbanda and Candomblé and other animistic practices of this region. He will help the magician understand that these forms are a more urbanized and industrialized versions of Shamanism and thus how the elfin can translate shamanism into urban settings. Like Voudoun, these are syncrestic practices merging the beliefs of various cultures and this spirit can aid the fae in understanding elfin magic as it is reflected in various religions and magical traditions. Also, he can help the elf comprehend how to elevate any particular magical system to a more advanced state of spiritual realization. This Shining One is also adept in the making of magic wands, canes, and staffs and can inform the elfin how to create hir own and instill them with great power.

Ferfånal: Imbues It With Magic
AUGUST 11TH TO 20TH
MAGIC: FETISHISM

AREA: NORTHERN SOUTH AMERICA

CONSTELLATION: VÅSTARUVA, ANDROMEDA

PLANETARY ASSOCIATION: MARS

FAERIE ASSISTANTS: MADREMONTE

This Shining One can aid the elfin in animating spirit or infusing spirit into various fetishes, particularly if they are of the fae's own creation. She is assisted by the Madremonte, who are the protectors of forests, thus she will especially help those who plant or protect trees and withdraw her energy from any who unnecessarily cut them. She is also the patron of those who use the forest as a refuge and retreat and can help any to learn how to live harmoniously with and in the woods, thus she is the patron of Woods-craft and those who practice it.

Gyldåfål: On the Crags
AUGUST 21ST TO 31ST
MAGIC: MOUNTAIN MAGIC
AREA: WESTERN SOUTH AMERICA AND ARGENTINA
CONSTELLATION: ZILONA, URSA MAJOR
PLANETARY ASSOCIATION: JUPITER
FAERIE ASSISTANTS: JASY JATERE

Gyldåfål is the patron of the mountains and aids any who live in the mountains to understand their secrets. He is assisted by the elf-like, Jasy Jatere, the patron of the afternoon nap or siesta – so you can see he really is an elf. This Shining One is an especial protector of children and will wreck due karma on any who harm them. He is also the protector of monks, hermits and meditators who retreat to mountain caves and fastnesses, and all those who live in the mountain valleys and other isolated places. The mountains are a powerhouse of various rocks, minerals and crystals and thus he can also teach the elfin much about the power and the spiritual nature of mineralogy and gems.

AUGUST 1ST
Jyndrel: Incites Them to Take Action
MAGIC: CAULDRON OF REBIRTH
CONSTELLATION: FYR, VULPECULA
PLANETARY ASSOCIATION: SATURN
FAERIE ASSISTANTS: ALUX

This spirit arouses enthusiasm in those she guides, encouraging them to take action toward the realization of their visions and goals. Those who study under her develop the ability to arouse others, and thus some of them come to be known as firebrands or rabble-rousers.

Naturally, this power is an indication of growing leadership ability or charisma, not necessarily organizational ability, but the ability to inspire others and to influence them deeply. Alas, these elfin frequently need a second in command or executive secretary to keep things running smoothly and to take care of many of the practical details of their work.

AUGUST 2ND

Avoryl: Enlightening Presence

MAGIC: THE STONE OF THE LAND
CONSTELLATION: RYSTATA, CAELUM
PLANETARY ASSOCIATION: MERCURY
FAERIE ASSISTANTS: BLUE CROW

These elfin come to have a positive effect on those around them. As they mature in their power, people just feel better when they are around and they are often viewed as being very spiritual or holy beings.

Often this power is enhanced through their association with a particular area or energy spot on the earth. These elfin develop a powerful connection to the land and a reciprocal relationship with the spirits and elementals of the area they inhabit.

AUGUST 3RD

Urifyn: Then It All Changed

MAGIC: SHIELD OF LOVE AND PROTECTION
CONSTELLATION: SABÂRWA, AQUARIUS
PLANETARY ASSOCIATION: SUN
FAERIE ASSISTANTS: CAIPORA

The elfin studying under Urifyn are learning how to make

significant changes in their lives or the lives of others without creating trauma, upset and disharmony. They are developing the power of creating smooth transitions.

These elfin are thus often seen as positive examples of success in the world for they introduce the new without upsetting the old. Their real trick is in making it all so inviting that others are eager to cooperate with them. Among the many things they are good at doing, advertising and public relations stand out.

AUGUST 4TH

Jevyndre: I Have Much to Accomplish

MAGIC: THE MAGIC MIRROR
CONSTELLATION: NALON, CORVUS
PLANETARY ASSOCIATION: URANUS
FAERIE ASSISTANTS: CAMAHUETO

The elfin born under this spirit come into this life feeling that there is something they must do or accomplish to succeed as spirits in this lifetime. They often feel a profound sense of urgency about this and this urgency frequently is applied to their everyday tasks and jobs, as though every little thing is vital and important and needs to be done now. In time, they see their true purpose and then they switch to applying all their energy toward its accomplishment. Needless to say, they can seem quite obsessed at times.

> *THE MORE WE BECOME LIKE THE SHINING ONES, THE MORE WE TEND TO GLOW.*

August 5th

Pyndara: Born Ready

MAGIC: THE RINGS OF POWER

CONSTELLATION: ALDAR, SERPENS

PLANETARY ASSOCIATION: SATURN

FAERIE ASSISTANTS: TRAUCO

These elfin come into this life with new powers that they are ready and eager to try out and use. They can be very determined and serious individuals, particularly when they are young, and may seem inordinately organized or mature beyond their years.

Because of their advanced status they can have a tendency and power to dominate others and need to be careful that they do not violate the true will and free choice of those others for to do so would be to fall in with the dark powers that seek to control all things for their exclusive benefit. Thus this life is in many ways a test for these elfin where they must choose between pursuing the way of the Seelie or Unseelie, the path of liberation or of dominance.

August 6th

Hylynde: Growing More Beautiful Every Day

MAGIC: SPEAR OF LIGHT AND DESTINY

CONSTELLATION: ROCHILA, PEGASUS

PLANETARY ASSOCIATION: MARS

FAERIE ASSISTANTS: ENCANTADO

The elfin who come under this spirit's aegis are learning to be beautiful and through the course of their lives, if they follow this spirit's guidance with devotion, will become increasingly more attractive. Part of the realization that this spirit imparts is that the spirit world impresses the material world, thus having a great personality not only is more attractive than mere physical beauty, but also, in time, transforms the material body and the DNA it is based upon.

August 7th

Jidordyn: I Have More than Enough Time

MAGIC: CAULDRON OF ABUNDANCE, CORNUCOPIA
CONSTELLATION: ACANTHA, CIRCINUS
PLANETARY ASSOCIATION: SUN
FAERIE ASSISTANTS: PILLAN

Jidordyn teaches these elfin to take their time. They are learning to be at ease, move with grace, hang back and let things develop on their own, confident in thems'elves and their destiny. This spirit will also reveal how this casual attitude not only is very attractive romantically, but also increases these elves power to attract luck and success to thems'elves.

Because of this increasing power, these elfin generally become generous individuals and this further increases their attractiveness and good fortune.

August 8th

Sorynsa: So They Tell Me

MAGIC: SHIELD OF LOVE AND PROTECTION
CONSTELLATION: SABÅRWA, AQUARIUS
PLANETARY ASSOCIATION: SUN
FAERIE ASSISTANTS: KUARAHY JÁRA

These elfin are learning the power of discrimination, especially that of determining truth from falsehood and reality from fantasy. They are taught how to listen with an open mind, discern the truth without confronting or necessarily pointing out the false or the foolish. They smile, they nod their understanding, but they do not necessarily agree. They are hard to dupe and hesitant to criticize. Thus they are learning to move smoothly through the world without arousing opposition or wasting their time pursuing dead ends.

August 9th

Donådor: Right on Target

MAGIC: CAULDRON OF REBIRTH
CONSTELLATION: FOLI, LYRA
PLANETARY ASSOCIATION: ASTEROIDS
FAERIE ASSISTANTS: WERE-ALLIGATORS

The elfin under the influence of this Shining One are developing the ability to be at the right place at the right time and while this may seem like luck to others, it is actually a power that they are exercising. They are especially good at getting in things at the beginning, on the ground floor so to speak, that is recognizing those ventures that will be successful and joining them or investing at the very start.

They also develop the ability to revitalize flagging enterprises, see what they need to change in order to turn things around and thus they make good management advisors.

MOST FOLKS WANT TO BELIEVE IN SOMETHING BIGGER AND GREATER THAN THEMSELVES. WE ELVES SIMPLY WISH TO KNOW THE TRUTH.

August 10th

Tifynre: Steps into the Future

MAGIC: FAERY CIRCLE
CONSTELLATION: FROHAMËL, COMA BERENICES
PLANETARY ASSOCIATION: PLUTO
FAERIE ASSISTANTS: HOMBRE GATO

The elfin born under this spirit are here to bring the future into the present. These, as they evolve, are the ones who will introduce new things into the world or society, ever seeking to improve what is currently happening. Because of this they are frequently fans of science fiction.

These elfin are eager to stir things up and are willing to face social criticism and even ostracism to bring about what they deem to be improved circumstances for the individuals in society. They become courageous individuals who will even face torture or death to achieve their goals and will literally bend over backwards in their quest for a better world.

August 11th

Nearle: Emerges from Hiding

MAGIC: HORN OF CALLING
CONSTELLATION: EQALO, CETUS
PLANETARY ASSOCIATION: JUPITER
FAERIE ASSISTANTS: YARA

Under Nearle's guidance, these elfin begin to come out of the closet, or out of the deep forest if you will. They have spent lifetimes hiding their faerie/elfin natures and now in this lifetime they are making a determination about being more open and revealing their true nature to the world or remaining in hiding. This is still a decision they have to make both about revealing their nature and how much to reveal, but usually they feel the call of others of our kind very strongly and are impressed by these kindred's courage in living as their true s'elves in the world, which greatly encourages them.

August 12th
Wizynre: Wants to Know the Reasons Why
Magic: The Stone of the Land
Constellation: Prasugae, Lupus
Planetary Association: Venus
Faerie Assistants: Ngen

Wizynre teaches the power of understanding inner motivations and thus these elfin can become impressive psychiatrists, psychologists and sorcerers. They are also those elfin who, as scientists, wish to understand how the Universe really came about and, as metaphysicians, seek to comprehend the true roots of life, being and consciousness.

Naturally, these elfin are interested in the secret forces that move the world, as well as the contents of their own psyche and the unconscious aspects of their being.

August 13th
Qidåle: Resists Dark Magic
Magic: The Stone of the Land
Constellation: Atarold, Monoceros
Planetary Association: Pluto
Faerie Assistants: Ngen-kütral

These elfin are becoming powerful protectors of the land and are learning to shield their realms from negative astral forces that may assault them. This spirit teaches them the power of wards, banishings and exorcisms and thus they often explore the techniques of shamanism or the various priesthoods.

Those born here have the power to bring judgment down upon those who delve into the dark but they are also here to learn the power of mercy, compassion and discrimination for often those who do dark magics do so unwittingly and this needs to be taken into account.

AUGUST 14TH

Toånvor: Stirring it Up

MAGIC: THE STONE OF THE LAND
CONSTELLATION: LACATAR, LEO MINOR
PLANETARY ASSOCIATION: PLUTO
FAERIE ASSISTANTS: TIUH TIUH

Toånvor shows those under his care how their catalytic natures will set things in motion without them doing anything more than being their own s'elves. He will further instruct them how to use this latent power effectively so that the changes they initiate begin to suggest direction and don't merely stir things up without purpose, which is what happens until they get a grip on their powers. Until then they are like individuals who throw a deck of cards in the air and let them fall where they may. In time, they become the mysterious magicians who throw the cards in the air only to have the ones they selected land face upward.

> THE SHINING ONES DON'T HAVE AURAS, THEY ARE AURAS.

AUGUST 15ᵀᴴ

Werdyn: Walks Silently

MAGIC: SWORD OF TRUTH AND JUSTICE
CONSTELLATION: SETÅTRU, OPHIUCUS
PLANETARY ASSOCIATION: URANUS
FAERIE ASSISTANTS: AI APAEC

Most don't see these elfin coming. They are frequently underestimated by those who encounter them until they do indeed work their magic and then everyone is amazed at what they've done, realizing, often when it is too late, that they were very wrong about their opinion concerning these elves.

These elfin learn to use surprise as a tool of their magic and thus can appear very humble and modest as they wait for the moment to act. Do not be fooled by their reticent demeanor; they are much more powerful than they appear. They are in the process of developing the power of invisibility.

AUGUST 16ᵀᴴ

Ridyndre: Sees the Possibilities

MAGIC: SPEAR OF LIGHT AND DESTINY
CONSTELLATION: SARTH, VELA
PLANETARY ASSOCIATION: EARTH
FAERIE ASSISTANTS: NGEN-KO

Ridyndre aids those born here to see the possibilities, particularly to discern the practical steps to making things better in their lives. These are not mere visionaries who see the future and what can be but have no idea how to get there. These elfin learn to perceive the very immediate future as well as the more distant possibilities and how to connect the two with concerted action.

Because of this, these elfin are often sought out as problem solvers, for their keen insight enables them to figure the way out of nearly any problem.

AUGUST 17ᵀᴴ
Ravydre: Sea Skimmer

MAGIC: THE MAGIC MIRROR
CONSTELLATION: HOLVORO, FORNAX
PLANETARY ASSOCIATION: MERCURY
FAERIE ASSISTANTS: NGEN-KÜRÜF

Beside frequently having a thing for water, these elfin achieve a keen ability to understand and reflect the feelings and emotions of those around them and to communicate, using energized feeling, a sense of understanding and simpatico. They can be very good therapists because people instinctively feel that they really understand and sympathize, which as they become more and more adept they are increasingly able to do.

Part of the lessons of this placement is to become non-judgmental, to empathize without inwardly criticizing or feeling superior to others.

AUGUST 18ᵀᴴ
Ulefa: Moon Magic

MAGIC: SACRED POOL
CONSTELLATION: FADON LUPRAE, CANIS MAJOR
PLANETARY ASSOCIATION: MOON
FAERIE ASSISTANTS: TAWADI

This birth position often attracts those who delve deeply into witchcraft in its various forms and is associated particularly with moon magic. This spirit teaches the elfin born here how to make the most effective use of the cycles of the moon to achieve what they wish in the world or in relationships.

These elfin are learning how to approach success in a step-by-step fashion closely observing the interior rhythms of those with whom they interact.

AUGUST 19ᵀᴴ

Golefyn: Found the Source
MAGIC: SWORD OF TRUTH AND JUSTICE
CONSTELLATION: ATAROLD, MONOCEROS
PLANETARY ASSOCIATION: MARS
FAERIE ASSISTANTS: NGEN-KURA

These elfin are potentially extremely powerful for they have reached to the source of magic and now have to bring that energy back into the world without overly upsetting the world or their own inner being. These can have a tendency to burn the candle at both ends, for they are often incredibly passionate, and because they are channeling such profound power face the danger of burning thems'elves out. These elves are in the process of higher initiation and this life is a crucible for them. Meditation and other calming exercises can be very helpful for these fae.

> THE BEGINNING HOLDS ALL THAT COMES AFTER. THE END CONTAINS ALL THAT CAME BEFORE. TIME IS ETERNAL AND IT IS ALWAYS NOW.

August 20th
Jyndarfe: In the Secret Place
MAGIC: STAFF OF POWER
CONSTELLATION: FOCIDA, CHAMALEON
PLANETARY ASSOCIATION: VENUS
FAERIE ASSISTANTS: MILKBIRD

Jyndarfe welcomes elfin into the inner circle where greater secrets will be revealed to them but also where there will be greater expectations of them. These elfin are being raised up in this life and advanced to a new level of power and authority.

With this increased power, however, comes greater privilege, increased protection but also the scrutiny and observation from the Shining Ones who are grooming these elfin for even greater responsibility. At the same time, much healing can occur in this lifetime as well as real opportunities to relax and enjoy. This spirit teaches these elfin that it is not all about work.

August 21st
Cäládar: Born of Opportunity
MAGIC: FAERY CIRCLE
CONSTELLATION: NERON, MENSA
PLANETARY ASSOCIATION: MARS
FAERIE ASSISTANTS: NGEN-MAWIDA

These elfin are being given an opportunity in this life that they have not necessarily earned; however, the Shining Ones, none-the-less, believe that they will rise to the occasion and live up to the potential they see in them.

Sometimes these elfin feel a bit out of place, like a child that has skipped a grade, but in time they will adjust to their new status and although it may require a bit of struggle the expectation is that they will master these new skills and powers and rise even higher.

August 22ⁿᵈ

Gålålynde: Fire Dragon Rises

MAGIC: CAULDRON OF ABUNDANCE, CORNUCOPIA
CONSTELLATION: WILDRONAE, CANES VENATICI
PLANETARY ASSOCIATION: MOON
FAERIE ASSISTANTS: NGEN-KULLIÑ

The elfin born here may have a thing for fire, certainly they can feel great power rising within them at times and as they become more adept they learn that these are not just unknown and strange feelings but true power that can be directed toward the realization of their goals. However, they may have a tendency to burn thems'elves out quickly, like a meteor, or be prone to manic phases, but with this spirit's aid they learn to pace thems'elves so their power endures and is not immediately consumed and wasted. They are on the path of pyromagery and in time come to see that the most potent and powerful fire is the inner fire of spirit.

August 23ʳᵈ

Glafin: For the Sake of All

MAGIC: SACRED POOL
CONSTELLATION: GATH, CRUX
PLANETARY ASSOCIATION: SATURN
FAERIE ASSISTANTS: NGEN-RÜPÜ

Gladin teaches willing servers who have dedicated thems'elves toward the greater good and these very often have a tendency to be involved in various causes. Two important lessons come with this place, the first is that it is better to live for the cause than die for it, and the second is that unless absolutely necessary the small should not be sacrificed for the larger or the individual for the group.

These elfin are evolving the ability to be attuned to the mass of humanity or sense the overall feelings and trends of the group to which they belong. Like porpoises in the sea, they are developing a sonic psychic sense that can communicate over far distances.

AUGUST 24TH

Perdynver: Quiet Moment

MAGIC: CAULDRON OF ABUNDANCE, CORNUCOPIA
CONSTELLATION: ARAK, SAGITTARIUS
PLANETARY ASSOCIATION: URANUS
FAERIE ASSISTANTS: PIRANU

Perdynver guides those in her care to achieve a quiet appreciation of life, particularly those silent sacred moments when one is at peace and everything seems to be going exactly as it should. In fact, despite whatever confusion or chaos the world seems to be in, these elfin come to see the underlying harmony of life and thus become a positive force for calm in a hectic world. As they become increasingly adept, they seem utterly unperturbed by anything occurring in the world and others tend to cling to them for guidance and support.

> *WE ELVES BELIEVE IN EDUCATION THE SAME AS WE BELIEVE IN LIFE. IT GOES ON FOREVER.*

AUGUST 25TH

Jinoryn: I Love to Sit and Watch the Sea

MAGIC: THE STONE OF THE LAND
CONSTELLATION: JUFI, OCTANS
PLANETARY ASSOCIATION: NEPTUNE
FAERIE ASSISTANTS: NGENECHEN

These elfin are often quite poetic in nature and thus you may find them writing poetry, songs or lyric literature. As they progress they come to be seen as being wise and to have some secret knowledge to which others don't have access. In the ancient days, they would be bards, ovates and druids or others of that kind. As they evolve they will have the ability to use their voice to draw energy up from the land or sea beneath them and to direct that power toward the realization of their visions.

AUGUST 26TH

Wifordyn: Wanders through Faerie

MAGIC: CAULDRON OF REBIRTH
CONSTELLATION: ARANDUS, RETICULUM
PLANETARY ASSOCIATION: JUPITER
FAERIE ASSISTANTS: NGEN-LAWEN

These elfin are advancing in their connection to Faerie in this life and as their lives progress they will find that they not only attract more and more of our kind but tend to find thems'elves in environments that are increasingly attuned to and expressive of Faerie.

These elfin become very radiant beings who absorb this elfin energy and express it outwardly inspiring others with their vibrant being. Naturally, they experience a great deal of luck, déjà vu and synchronicities in their lives.

August 27th

Sidynde: Sits with the Elves
MAGIC: SHIELD OF LOVE AND PROTECTION
CONSTELLATION: RYNGYL, APUS
PLANETARY ASSOCIATION: SATURN
FAERIE ASSISTANTS: NGEN-WINGKUL

These elfin are in the process of becoming very group or community oriented and as they evolve they become ever more comfortable being an individual among other strong individuals. Often they feel estranged from the world in general but in their elven artists community they become confident and secure.

Often these fae are faced with the difference between living in the idealized and more utopian worlds they have created and the less evolved world around them and somehow having to find a compromise between them.

August 28th

Kelormyn: It's the Way it Happened
MAGIC: SPEAR OF LIGHT AND DESTINY
CONSTELLATION: UNTWON, GEMINI
PLANETARY ASSOCIATION: MOON
FAERIE ASSISTANTS: IMPUNDULU

These elfin are very truth and fact oriented and can have a keen interest in history or being historians. They usually want the facts behind the story or the facts behind the facts. They know that history is written by the victors and they are well aware that much of the truth, if not most of it, is covered up and airbrushed for posterity thus these elfin learn to look at life as they know it and use their creative imaginations to project basic human nature into the past to gain a greater understanding of the circumstances of their ancestors while, at the same time, keeping in mind that their projections are merely theories.

August 29th

Feåvae: Eyes Alive
MAGIC: STAFF OF POWER
CONSTELLATION: ELPAN, CAMELOPARDALIS
PLANETARY ASSOCIATION: URANUS
FAERIE ASSISTANTS: KURUPI

This spirit teaches the elfin under his care how to channel light through their eyes, how to accumulate energy with their eyes, how to send messages and suggestions to others through them and much more on the magic of the eyes that are the mirrors of the soul. Quite often the eyes of these elfin seem to sparkle.

These elfin work with powers that are for the most part unseen by any but adepts of this art. Naturally, these elfin are increasingly able to see into the astral realms, see auras and other aspects of being that go unnoticed by normal folk.

Those who rewrite history in an attempt to fool others wind up deceiving themselves.
—Old Elven Saying

AUGUST 30ᵀᴴ

Ilele: Hazy Dawn

MAGIC: FAERY CIRCLE
CONSTELLATION: ATAROLD, MONOCEROS
PLANETARY ASSOCIATION: PLUTO
FAERIE ASSISTANTS: NGEN-MAPU

While these elfin frequently have confused childhoods and teenage years, their life takes on ever-greater direction and form as they progress. Their early life is like a storm, their later life the calm after the storm, thus these elfin can be seen as having experienced or endured a lot very early in life.

Because of these early experiences, however, these elfin acquire a deep inner power that they can draw on when needed, and while they may seem calm most of the time can be fearsome if aroused.

AUGUST 31ˢᵀ

Melefyn: Moonlight Serenade

MAGIC: SHIELD OF LOVE AND PROTECTION
CONSTELLATION: TOLOTO, CARINA
PLANETARY ASSOCIATION: MOON
FAERIE ASSISTANTS: CURUPIRA

These elfin are under the protection of occult powers in this lifetime and are being introduced to the netherworlds and the realms and dimensions that others seldom encounter and quickly erase from their memories if they do. Melefyn helps these elfin become accustomed to the fact that greater forces are moving their lives and that psychic impressions will frequently arise within them and may at times seem overwhelming. Part of what this spirit does is help these elfin develop strong mental powers and an independence of spirit that enables them to listen in or tune out these impressions at will.

> THE SHINING ONES LIVE AMONG THE STARS BUT THEY ALSO LIVE AMONG THE TREES OF THE FOREST, THE ROCKS OF THE HIGH MOUNTAINS AND THE WAVES OF THE OCEAN DEEP.

> WE ELVES ARE ALCHEMISTS. WE MIX LOVE WITH HAPPINESS AND SMILES, AND CREATE MAGIC.
> —OLD ELVEN KNOWLEDGE

> DESCRIBING ELVES IS LIKE DESCRIBING THE SHIMMERING HUES OF A RAINBOW.

SEPTEMBER

RYNVATHEYL: AMONG THE TREES

MONTH: SEPTEMBER

MAGIC: DRUIDRY

CONTINENT: EUROPE

CONSTELLATION: GATH, CRUX

PLANETARY ASSOCIATION: VENUS

FAERIE ASSISTANTS: GNOMES

Rynvatheyl, with the assistance of the Gnomes, teaches and protects Druids and all those who learn from the trees. She is the patron of those born in or living in Europe or of European descent. She also rules the seas and anything that happens near rivers, lakes or oceans comes under her purview. Thus trees near rivers or lakes are her special province. All Faerie folk that are near these areas may evoke her with confidence.

Odånådal: In the Forest
SEPTEMBER 1ST AND 10TH
MAGIC: TREE MAGIC
AREA: IRELAND AND BRITISH ISLES
CONSTELLATION: ORMYN, CENTAURUS
PLANETARY ASSOCIATION: PLUTO
FAERIE ASSISTANTS: LEPRECHAUNS

Odånådal, with the assistance of the Leprechauns, is a master of tree magic including how to use a tree to communicate through the underground water system to other trees at far distances. Odånådal also has a white raven as a companion and is noted for her frequent travels, thus she is a patron of travelers. She further has a relationship with the Wise Old Salmon and can teach the willing magician much about the wisdom of the soul and psychic communication.

Givynthal: Poetic Spells
SEPTEMBER 11TH TO 20TH
MAGIC: BARDIC MAGIC

AREA: WESTERN EUROPE

CONSTELLATION: LUTRA, PISCES

PLANETARY ASSOCIATION: ASTEROIDS

FAERIE ASSISTANTS: WALDGEIST

The Waldgeist, or woodspirits who are related to the Dryads, Wood Nymphs, and other tree spirits, assist this Shining One who is a Master Bard and is a patron of all lyricists, poets, rhymers and others who delve in rhyming spells. He is also an inspirer of lovers and is noted as a matchmaker, and a patron of matchmakers, who bring together those whose union will bring success and be beneficial to all parties concerned. He is an extremely active spirit and is constantly on the look out for those with the least bit of talent in poetry and encourages every effort made in this regard.

THEY SAY THAT THOSE THAT CAN DO AND THOSE THAT CAN'T TEACH. YET WE ELVES TEACH BY DOING, LEAD BY EXAMPLE AND LEARN FROM ALL WE DO.

Omerpal: Finds Fresh Water
SEPTEMBER 21ST TO 30TH
MAGIC: WATER WITCHING
AREA: EASTERN EUROPE AND WESTERN RUSSIA
CONSTELLATION: LOWA, ERIDANUS
PLANETARY ASSOCIATION: ASTEROIDS
FAERIE ASSISTANTS: ZHAR-PTITSA

Omerpal, is aided by the Zhar-Ptitsa or Fire-bird that is another form of the Phoenix. This Shining One is an expert at water witching or using the forked branch and other means to find water sources underground. Because of this, Omerpal is also an aid to those who feel stuck in life and are searching for a way out of their current state of ennui, boredom or unchanging mundane circumstances. He can guide one in a step by step fashion in taking the magical actions that will open the pathway to new opportunities and thus to rise above one's circumstance into more exalted levels of magical interaction.

SEPTEMBER 1ST

Usyrnyn: They Need a Little Guidance
MAGIC: HORN OF CALLING
CONSTELLATION: MATH, PYXIS
PLANETARY ASSOCIATION: URANUS
FAERIE ASSISTANTS: GREEN CHILDREN

The elfin born here are near the point where they can proceed totally on their own in their evolutionary course, but just need a little bit more guidance, some last minute/lifetime polishing up and refinement. They are near to graduation on their current level of being.

These elfin are seizing control of their own destiny, they usually have a strong ally in the natural world that serves as their companion/ally and have developed the ability to summon elementals to fulfill their will; thus they are becoming powerful conjurers.

September 2ⁿᵈ

Widyndre: Wanders the Woods Seeking Magic

MAGIC: STAFF OF POWER
CONSTELLATION: VÅSTARUVA, ANDROMEDA
PLANETARY ASSOCIATION: URANUS
FAERIE ASSISTANTS: SELKIES

Widyndre teaches sympathetic magic, particularly the magic of analogies and how to use anything found in nature as an ingredient in one's spells. These elfin are frequently into hedgewitchery, doing small magics for success and to help others in the world, thus they tend to be very practical beings.

Often these elfin are very tenacious spirits who are usually found with a familiar, a dog, cat, bird or other creature as their constant companion. These creatures are absolutely loyal to them and will die to protect them and to extend their lives. This is a mystery of magical association and their willing sacrifice is rewarded in their next life.

ELVES SELDOM SPEAK OF PUNISHMENT OR RETRIBUTION BUT RATHER OF BALANCE, HEALING, AND FAIRNESS.

SEPTEMBER 3ʳᴰ

Uthela: They Remained Behind

MAGIC: CAULDRON OF ABUNDANCE, CORNUCOPIA
CONSTELLATION: RIFRO, PHOENIX
PLANETARY ASSOCIATION: MOON
FAERIE ASSISTANTS: PECHS

Uthela helps guide those elfin who have had a chance to progress onward, even move to other dimensions, but have decided to remain on this plane to help those that they love and for whom they feel a responsibility. In this way, they have already undertaken the work of the Shining Ones.

Because of their advanced status and evolutionary development these elfin are frequently seers who have great knowledge of the past and the inclinations of individuals as they develop into the future. This gives them an advantage in dealing with the material world where they can be quite successful.

SEPTEMBER 4ᵀᴴ

Pirunyn: Rare Chance

MAGIC: THE MAGIC MIRROR
CONSTELLATION: LACATAR, LEO MINOR
PLANETARY ASSOCIATION: SUN
FAERIE ASSISTANTS: PIXIES

The elfin born here are offered a rare opportunity to gain powers and knowledge that are not usually shared. Because of this there is a basic sense that there is something very special about these beings and an expectation that they will do something important for the development of the faery race.

These elfin have usually endured a lot in their previous lives, have seen their hopes crushed again and again and have learned to persevere despite this. This suffering was needed to develop these powers and now that they have them they are rewarded with an opportunity to do something truly great and profound.

SEPTEMBER 5ᵀᴴ

Arynthel: As Best You Can
MAGIC: THE STONE OF THE LAND
CONSTELLATION: PRASUGAE, LUPUS
PLANETARY ASSOCIATION: EARTH
FAERIE ASSISTANTS: HULDRA

All that Arynthel asks is that those under his care do their very best and if they do so they will be rewarded with luck and success. These elfin are well aware of having progressed through the various stages of evolution. They have been rocks, trees, fish, birds and so on and carry the experience of those lifetimes within and are able to call forth these energies when needed in the world.

In this life, they are learning the power of rhyme, vibration and resonance and thus have a proclivity toward poetry and song as well as rhyming spells, thus they are often attracted to Buddhist or other chanting magics.

SEPTEMBER 6ᵀᴴ

Vëlide: True to the Spirit
MAGIC: HORN OF CALLING
CONSTELLATION: ELFASA, DELPHINUS
PLANETARY ASSOCIATION: NEPTUNE
FAERIE ASSISTANTS: SJÖRÅ

This Shining One helps those under her care to attune to the spirit of Faerie and become resonate vibrations of that spirit. Because of this others seeking faerie naturally gravitate toward these individuals.

It is as though these elfin have a scent, like a fragrant flower, that draws others to them. The appeal they have is mostly subliminal and this power will continually increase as they mature. What they will do with these individuals when they come is something these fae are still figuring out in this lifetime.

September 7th

Jåmarys: Hill Climber

MAGIC: CAULDRON OF ABUNDANCE, CORNUCOPIA
CONSTELLATION: KOFI, COLUMBA
PLANETARY ASSOCIATION: URANUS
FAERIE ASSISTANTS: SILKIES

Those born here often have a resonance with the hills and mountains, thus they are frequently rock or mountain climbers, and are learning to draw power from these regions. This spirit also teaches the use of minerals and crystals for spiritual development and magic and thus these elfin sometimes have an interest in the lapidary arts and work with precious metals or other minerals that bring them material success.

Because of their propensity for prosperity, as well as their youthful enthusiasm, these individuals often seem younger than they are and filled with vibrant energy.

LADY LUCK IS AN ELF.

September 8th

Aride: Dances Amidst the Starlight

MAGIC: THE MAGIC MIRROR
CONSTELLATION: LUTRA, PISCES
PLANETARY ASSOCIATION: MARS
FAERIE ASSISTANTS: DOOINNEY-OIE

Aride teaches those under her care to weave starlight into spells creating worlds of magic. These are on the path to Star Enchantment and will oversee solar systems and galaxies in the future.

These elfin learn the power of seeing things anew, with a fresh point of view as a child sees things. They are thus very resistant to peer pressure. This attainment of child-like innocence with increasing maturity is the path to wisdom and these elfin come to understand in time what every person needs and desires.

September 9th

Uzara: At Peace with Ones'elf

MAGIC: STAFF OF POWER
CONSTELLATION: IRANALI, PICTOR
PLANETARY ASSOCIATION: SATURN
FAERIE ASSISTANTS: HAVSRÅ

Uzara shows those born here the ways to finding inner peace and calm, particularly coming to have an inner sense of well-being and acceptance and appreciation of one's own nature.

These elfin are further developing healing powers, their own calm having a soothing effect on others around them that helps allay the stress that is the source of so many diseases. When they are fully adept in this power they become a calm center around which the world spins.

SEPTEMBER 10TH

Udyntha: Tells the Ancient Stories
MAGIC: THE RINGS OF POWER
CONSTELLATION: ZILONA, URSA MAJOR
PLANETARY ASSOCIATION: MARS
FAERIE ASSISTANTS: BERGSRÅ

Here is a place of tale-tellers, legend keepers, and story creators. These elfin learn how to tap into the Collective Unconscious of the Faerie Race and to translate our mythology into tales that serve as illustrations for problem solving in the modern world. This is a place of great power for those who shape the mythology of a people, who in this way shape their future.

These elfin may use this power in various ways, expressing their vision in song, fantasy or philosophy but the key to their power is their ability to arouse the mysterious and awaken the imagination.

SEPTEMBER 11TH

Olefyn: Passion for Romance
MAGIC: SACRED POOL
CONSTELLATION: LARCA, LEO
PLANETARY ASSOCIATION: SATURN
FAERIE ASSISTANTS: VÆTTIR

The elfin born under this spirit's guidance have come in this lifetime to learn the ability to channel passion, especially romantic passion, toward the fulfillment of their magic. This does not mean that they give up interest in romance, quite the contrary for they become masters of the romantic arts in the course of time, but that they learn to moderate and intensify this energy and use it as they will. Thus they are frequently practitioners of Tantra.

The greatest use of this power, however, is one of personal transformation and when these elfin have finished this course of study they shine as beings with tremendous discipline and s'elf control that they can direct toward anything they desire.

SEPTEMBER 12TH

Ziredyn: Worth Doing Well

MAGIC: SHIELD OF LOVE AND PROTECTION
CONSTELLATION: ALDAR, SERPENS
PLANETARY ASSOCIATION: ASTEROIDS
FAERIE ASSISTANTS: AUGHISKY

Ziredyn reveals the power of perfection. The motto: *if it is worth doing it is worth doing well*, applies to this course of evolutionary instruction. Thus the elfin born here are often specialists in one area or another, concentrating, at least in this lifetime, on the things they need to perfect and serving as protectors of these things. Thus they are frequently artisans or craftspeople preserving and passing on the secrets of their trade to those who are truly interested.

These elfin are often very passionate about these interests, they may even be seen to be obsessed about them, but this is as it needs to be so they can fully concentrate on their work.

SOMETIMES YOU JUST HAVE TO DANCE.
—OLD ELVEN SAYING

SEPTEMBER 13TH

Jilenyn: I Insist on what Is Right
MAGIC: HORN OF CALLING
CONSTELLATION: FAERO, TRIANGULUM
PLANETARY ASSOCIATION: JUPITER
FAERIE ASSISTANTS: WITTE WIEVEN

The elfin born here are learning to get it right. Jilenyn can seem a hard task-master but when he is done these fae will be experts in their chosen fields of magical study and masters of their powers. He can also, however, be quite generous to those who progress and will grant them wishes for each level they master.

Once these elfin have gained mastery, they can pursue their heart's desire with great power and with confidence of success. However, they do tend to be somewhat exacting spirits who will not settle for second best.

SEPTEMBER 14TH

Zådilyn: Wishes to Know the Truth
MAGIC: HORN OF CALLING
CONSTELLATION: ROCHILA, PEGASUS
PLANETARY ASSOCIATION: NEPTUNE
FAERIE ASSISTANTS: HABETROT

The truth, the whole truth and nothing but the truth appeals to these elfin. They tend to be non-fiction readers, but when they do read fiction they expect the worlds they read about, even if they are fantasy or science fiction, to make sense and be internally coherent. It is these elves who watch movies and point out all the discrepancies and inconsistencies. Some might think these folks have no imagination, however, quite the opposite it true, their imagination is so evolved that it takes in every detail and they expect those details to be coherent.

These are often very old elfin spirits who carry with them the blessings of the ancestors and are guided by them.

September 15th

Dorthålyn: Feels Them Beckoning

MAGIC: SPEAR OF LIGHT AND DESTINY
CONSTELLATION: PAVOCA, PAVO
PLANETARY ASSOCIATION: MERCURY
FAERIE ASSISTANTS: DWARVES

Those born here tend to feel the call of Faerie very strongly and are eager to make swift and sure progress in their evolutionary development. They become very determined beings and are not easy to sway through peer pressure or societal enculturation.

Because of their close association with the Faerie realms, they have a propensity to radiate fairy energies in all that they do and with that the sense that they have some mysterious power that lends them success and luck in their lives. In fact, this seeming luck arises usually from a great deal of hard work and is well earned.

September 16th

Fearve: Eyes that Sparkle

MAGIC: THE MAGIC MIRROR
CONSTELLATION: HELON, SCUTUM
PLANETARY ASSOCIATION: JUPITER
FAERIE ASSISTANTS: CLURICAUNE

Fearve help these elfin develop their inner radiance, the power of their souls and the result of this is that their eyes often seem to glow or sparkle. These elfin are also on the path to being wish granters and when they bless others, those others are truly lucky.

These elfin are inwardly strong and make powerful and reliable allies. Those who call them friend are blessed indeed. At the same time, they have a mysterious aura and tend to be quiet or seemingly shy, thus many folks underestimate them.

SEPTEMBER 17TH

Zilynde: World Maker

MAGIC: FAERY CIRCLE
CONSTELLATION: FROHAMÈL, COMA BERENICES
PLANETARY ASSOCIATION: MARS
FAERIE ASSISTANTS: URISKS

Zilynde instructs those in his realm about the elements of world building. These elfin are on the verge or in the process of creating their own ealds/demesnes and as they become more and more adept these realms will be larger and more intricate.

Since they are usually creating something new there is a sense of youthfulness and energy about these elfin. They often give one the sense that the whole world is being born anew and thus inspire others with hope.

THE SHINING ONES SAY WE WILL ALWAYS FIND THOSE WHO ARE MEANT FOR US IF WE TRUST OUR NATURAL ATTRACTIONS.

September 18th

Hylase: Growing Confident

Magic: Spear of Light and Destiny
Constellation: Rynd, Equuleus
Planetary Association: Saturn
Faerie Assistants: Iele

The elfin born under the direction of this Shining One are here to become increasing confident in thems'elves and in the course of this instruction find s'elf validation and approval growing with them. Sometimes they come from situations and lifetimes where it seemed that they were subject to constant criticism and were frequently looked down upon. Having passed that course, which was taken to develop compassion for the underdog, these elfin have grown strong through adversity and in this lifetime learn to divorce their sense of s'elf from the negative manipulations of others.

September 19th

Uberyn: Taking Care of Business

Magic: Shield of Love and Protection
Constellation: Focida, Chamaleon
Planetary Association: Venus
Faerie Assistants: Radande

These elfin are fierce protectors of those they love and often have come into this life specifically to serve as guardians and protectors of certain individuals. These fae can be quite dedicated spirits and are intent on achieving what they feel to be their mission in life. Often, however, once they have accomplished this they live out their lives under the grace of the Shining Ones and can pursue whatever quest they choose or simply enjoy their lives until their next life finds them pursuing a new course of study. Some might call them guardian angels; we call them guardian elfin.

September 20th
Onorys: Phantom Shadow
MAGIC: SWORD OF TRUTH AND JUSTICE
CONSTELLATION: RYNGYL, APUS
PLANETARY ASSOCIATION: MERCURY
FAERIE ASSISTANTS: DACTYLS

You may not notice these elfin or recognize the influence they have over others or the influence they have in your life but they are developing great powers and these are mostly used to evoke spells that are so subtle as to be invisible to most.

These elfin are usually faithful agents of higher powers and are dedicated to changing the world for the better, although it is unlikely they will get any credit in the world for what they have accomplished. However, no effort is ever lost and in the course of evolutionary development they will receive their just reward in increased powers and abilities.

September 21st
Denålynsa: Colors the World with Magic
MAGIC: SPEAR OF LIGHT AND DESTINY
CONSTELLATION: ZILONDAR, URSA MINOR
PLANETARY ASSOCIATION: MOON
FAERIE ASSISTANTS: ADHENE

Denålynsa teaches those under her influence the ways to subtly affect the world. These elfin use an accumulation of small, practically unnoticed changes to bring about larger transformations.

They develop foresight and are in the process of becoming visionaries, for these abilities are needed to comprehend the subtle magics that will create profound shifts in the world. They come to understand that the little things can make all the difference in life.

September 22nd

Viarde: Truth Teller

Magic: Cauldron of Rebirth
Constellation: Nalon, Corvus
Planetary Association: Neptune
Faerie Assistants: Brownies

These elfin are truth tellers, but what this Shining One imparts to them is the ways and means of giving the truth in such a fashion that it will be accepted and will not be unduly offensive. Thus these elfin learn to be particularly aware of the feelings of others, both how to help without hurting those feelings and how to arouse their deepest feelings that remind them of life in Faerie.

Naturally, these elfin have developed their own inner sensitivity and have great access to the inner well of inspiration and creativity.

September 23rd

Isylfyn: Hears the Dawn

Magic: Cauldron of Abundance, Cornucopia
Constellation: Nesnor, Norma
Planetary Association: Uranus
Faerie Assistants: Knockers

Isylfyn aids those under his aegis to develop clairvoyant abilities, especially to hear the inner thoughts and feelings of others as they are related to their aspirations and desires. For these elves, feelings speak and they listen. These elfin come to instinctively know what others truly wish to become and are able to assist them in their evolution.

This is a lifetime of flowering for these elfin and much that heretofore was coming into being on the unseen realms now emerges into the light, manifesting in their lives in the material world.

SEPTEMBER 24TH

Fynwedyn: Finds Joy in All Things

MAGIC: CAULDRON OF REBIRTH
CONSTELLATION: WYTRE, LIBRA
PLANETARY ASSOCIATION: PLUTO
FAERIE ASSISTANTS: COBLYNAU

The elfin in this evolutionary study group are learning the magic power of joy, how to evoke it, how to heal with it, how to summon it at will. This is a tremendous power that many who are still straining to be magicians overlook.

These elfin often have an association with the fire elementals for this power is enlivening and awakens the inner fire and by its nature seeks to spread and share itself. It burns away the sorrows of the past and awakens the spirit within. Thus these elfin are learning the techniques of pyromagery.

THE SHINING ONES SAY THE FIRST CAUSE IS OUR DESIRE TO BE WHOLE.

SEPTEMBER 25TH

Ilevyn: Dusky Dawn

MAGIC: THE MAGIC MIRROR
CONSTELLATION: SARTH, VELA
PLANETARY ASSOCIATION: MERCURY
FAERIE ASSISTANTS: PISKIES

These elfin are learning to find clarity in the midst of confusion. They are also here to learn to have faith and to understand that things are often difficult in the beginning; however, if they proceed with determination and perseverance problems will naturally clear up as things evolve. Thus these elfin are learning not to give up when they feel overwhelmed by the seemingly endless number of tasks they are called to complete.

Those born here are learning how to deal with fate, that is to say, the entangled circumstances of the world that reflects their karma, and to make the most of it, untangling each knotted spell as they encounter it.

SEPTEMBER 26TH

Ovånådyn: Power of the Will

MAGIC: THE MAGIC MIRROR
CONSTELLATION: DEOSA, CANCER
PLANETARY ASSOCIATION: PLUTO
FAERIE ASSISTANTS: OCEANIDS

This Shining One teaches the power of combined Will, that is to say elfin gathering together in covens and vortexes and using their wills in concert with each other for mutual benefit. This group energy raises these elfin higher than any one of them could reach alone and their ability to achieve what they wish as well as their evolutionary progress is heightened thereby. Together these elfin soar to new heights and they all profit from this cooperative effort.

SEPTEMBER 27TH
Nevere: On a Mission
MAGIC: STAFF OF POWER
CONSTELLATION: PRASUGAE, LUPUS
PLANETARY ASSOCIATION: ASTEROIDS
FAERIE ASSISTANTS: METSÄN VÄKI

The elfin born here have a mission to fulfill and usually are given heightened powers to achieve and fulfill it. Often these powers are not their own, that is to say they did not, as yet, earn them and these powers will not follow them from one life to another until they do earn them. However, like someone who has the power and authority of some office, like the powers of a president, they will be able to use these powers in this lifetime as long as they continue on this mission. And if they do successfully complete it, they will surely be rewarded for doing so. Although it should be pointed out that while in the material world those who try and fail are usually seen as losers, in the realms of spirit, every sincere effort rebounds to one's benefit.

SEPTEMBER 28TH
Jänådur: Hint of Magic
MAGIC: SHIELD OF LOVE AND PROTECTION
CONSTELLATION: TONENYS, PUPPIS
PLANETARY ASSOCIATION: EARTH
FAERIE ASSISTANTS: SAMODIVAS

This Shining One instructs those born here in the power of the hint, particularly as a teaching tool. Thus those born in this position are likely to become teachers of their chosen fields of magic in the future. In fact, a good many of them hold classes or aspire to teach metaphysics in this lifetime.

These elfin also learn the power of totems and how to use that power to enhance their own powers. This includes totem animals but it also covers totem figures and teraphim, household gods, and the use of idols.

SEPTEMBER 29TH
Milefyn: Music Fills My Soul

MAGIC: CAULDRON OF ABUNDANCE, CORNUCOPIA
CONSTELLATION: FROHAMĖL, COMA BERENICES
PLANETARY ASSOCIATION: MOON
FAERIE ASSISTANTS: TOMTE

Milefyn shows these elfin how music enhances one's life, touches the soul and thus arouses the imagination and magical power. These elfin come to understand the secrets of music as a source of abundance, making life richer and more profound, as well as using music as a means to impress and evoke memories.

These elfin learn how to empower music with messages that can reach out and touch those who hear it. Naturally, they are often musicians, songwriters and/or composers thems'elves.

WE ARE NOT ELVES BECAUSE OUR PARENTS WERE ELVES OR OUR ANCESTORS WERE ELVES BUT BECAUSE WE LOVE ALL THINGS ELVEN.

SEPTEMBER 30TH

Dåveryn: Clearer than Ice

MAGIC: SPEAR OF LIGHT AND DESTINY
CONSTELLATION: MIHAN, ORION
PLANETARY ASSOCIATION: JUPITER
FAERIE ASSISTANTS: DUENDE

Those born in this place are here to learn how to make things crystal clear. Once they do this they become very effective communicators who are seldom misunderstood and whose messages resonate deeply into the hearts and minds of others.

Often, these elfin come with a purpose. They have a message for humanity or a portion of humanity that they are here to communicate that will prove beneficial to those mature and wise enough to listen. They often feel driven to deliver this message, which they frequently perceive as a personal discovery and illumination, and feel a great satisfaction when others are able to use their information to advance thems'elves.

THE SHINING ONES ARE NOT DEMONS ONE CAN CONTROL OR ORDER ABOUT. THEY ARE MORE LIKE AN ECCENTRIC RELATIVE ONE HAS INVITED TO VISIT BUT WHO UNEXPECTEDLY SHOWS UP ON ONE'S DOORSTEP WITH A TWINKLE IN THEIR EYES AND A KNOWING SMILE ON THEIR LIPS.

> *The Shining Ones are not your parents, your aunt, uncle, cousins, brother, sister; but they very well may have been so in previous lifetimes.*

> *The Shining Ones can not be coerced, bribed, or commanded. They are, however, swayed by enchantment, which is what the elves are ever about.*

> *The ancient Elven magic is not contained in lost tomes but secreted in the hearts and souls of the elves.*

> *They say love makes the world go around. Thus the elves use love to create magic and magic to create love and in this way keep the great dance spinning.*

OCTOBER

SORYNTHÈL: MIXES THE HEALING HERBS

MONTH: OCTOBER

MAGIC: SHAMANISM AND HEALING

CONTINENT: GREENLAND, ICELAND, ARCTIC ALASKA, ARCTIC CANADA, LAPLAND AND SIBERIA

CONSTELLATION: ILDRA, LEPUS

PLANETARY ASSOCIATION: SATURN

FAERIE ASSISTANTS: REINDEER PEOPLE

This Shining One is assisted by the Reindeer People and is particularly a patron of all Eskimo tribes, all Laps and all Tundra peoples. These, of necessity, must be a hardy folk and Sorynthèl promotes endurance and strength in all whom she guides. If you are looking for the strength to endure hard times, she will assist you, although, you won't necessarily find it easy. She teaches one to thrive in harsh circumstances, even to find abundance in thrifty times. Her magic secrets are deep and must be earned.

THE SHINING ONES DO NOT REWARD US FOR DOING GOOD DEEDS OR PUNISH THOSE WHO ARE BAD*, BUT FAVOR THOSE WHO LIVE LIFE WITH SPIRIT, ELEGANCE AND STYLE.

* THAT IS THE WORK OF THE LORDS OF KARMA

Ivyndåra: Shapes the Ice
OCTOBER 1ST TO 10TH
MAGIC: ICE AND SNOW MAGIC

AREA: GREENLAND AND ICELAND

CONSTELLATION: ATAROLD, MONOCEROS

PLANETARY ASSOCIATION: SATURN

FAERIE ASSISTANTS: BERGSRÅ

Ivyndåra, with help from the Bergsrå or mountain spirits, is the master of Ice and Snow Magics. She is also a patron of artists who sculpt or shape ice. She often appears as a young girl with a white cat and takes delight in toys of various sorts. She can teach one to live in harsh environments and is naturally a guardian for all those who live above the artic circle or in snowy, frozen climes.

Donådal: Root Worker
OCTOBER 11TH TO 20TH
MAGIC: HERBALOGY, WORTCUNNING

AREA: ARCTIC ALASKA AND ARCTIC CANADA

CONSTELLATION: URMA, DORADO

PLANETARY ASSOCIATION: SUN

FAERIE ASSISTANTS: AGLOOLIK

The Agloolik, which is a water spirit that lives beneath the ice, is an aid to Donådal the root worker. This spirit rules Arctic Alaska and Canada, but his magical power includes root work and root working wherever it is found. All herbalists come under his influence. He is particularly adept, however, in teaching one how to find rare herbs or to find herbs in places where they are rare or hard to locate. He is also a master of using seaweed and other sea vegetation for magic and healing. He is a very tolerant spirit and particularly encouraging of those who are just beginning to study in his areas of expertise. He can also inspire one into new uses of herbs and roots than those traditionally known. You might think that the arctic is a strange place for a root worker, but here his powers are really put to the test.

Wivynfål: Persuades the Weather
OCTOBER 21ST TO 31ST

MAGIC: WEATHER WITCHING
AREA: LAPLAND AND SIBERIA
CONSTELLATION: WILDRONAE, CANES VENATICI
PLANETARY ASSOCIATION: PLUTO
FAERIE ASSISTANTS: ISHIGAQ

The Ishigaq are fairy folk of the snowy regions and are eager assistants to Wivynfål who is a master of controlling or altering the weather. Thus he is in great demand by hunters in the region he holds sway over. He can teach one much about changing the weather but also is a patron of weather forecasters. Additionally, he can instruct one in the understanding of microclimates, of seasons within seasons, and much more concerning the elements of weather magic. He is a very clever spirit and is more inclined to help the magician understand how it is easier to adapt to the changes of weather than to try to control it. He will further help the elf to understand the weather and the elements as spirits rather than as simple mechanical forces.

TO EVOKE THE SHINING ONES IS ULTIMATELY ALWAYS AN EVOCATION OF OUR OWN HIGHER SELF.

October 1ˢᵗ
Wifore: Wants It All to Work Out
MAGIC: CAULDRON OF ABUNDANCE, CORNUCOPIA
CONSTELLATION: SARTH, VELA
PLANETARY ASSOCIATION: VENUS
FAERIE ASSISTANTS: LJÓSÁLFAR

Wifore helps those in her care to create fairy tale endings to every situation. These elfin wish everything to work out perfectly with the Just getting their due and the Wicked learning a valuable lesson and this Shining One shows them how to recognize the steps that lead to this.

These elfin generally feel a strong connection to the ancestors and understand the ancient tales as valuable lessons in magic and a guide to proper living. They often hunger to reconnect with the past and bring it to life in the modern world.

October 2ⁿᵈ
Tyndåle: Sword Namer
MAGIC: SWORD OF TRUTH AND JUSTICE
CONSTELLATION: ZILONA, URSA MAJOR
PLANETARY ASSOCIATION: NEPTUNE
FAERIE ASSISTANTS: SJÖVÆTTIR

Those born here are learning to realize that all things are alive or can become vessels for spirits and thus they come to understand the magical power of names, especially giving names to swords, cars or other seemingly inanimate objects that can be spiritualized, that is to say filled or instilled with a particular spirit.

Thus these elfin learn that in empowering others, including the objects in their lives, they surround thems'elves with power that is available and accessible for their magic.

October 3ʳᵈ

Imydre: Healing Ways

MAGIC: FAERY CIRCLE
CONSTELLATION: ULOS, TAURUS
PLANETARY ASSOCIATION: URANUS
FAERIE ASSISTANTS: SVARTÁLFAR

Imydre shows those born here various modes of healing, especially faery healing, which includes such subtle magics as a kind smile and a loving attitude. These elfin seldom apply thems'elves to healing illness but rather put nearly all their energy toward preventing it. They create healing atmospheres so disease does not arise.

These elfin also learn the power of words to heal or harm and thus learn to become very careful in what they say and the tone or vibration with which they say it.

October 4ᵀᴴ

Yndåle: Strong Attraction

MAGIC: SWORD OF TRUTH AND JUSTICE
CONSTELLATION: VANUS, VOLANS
PLANETARY ASSOCIATION: VENUS
FAERIE ASSISTANTS: HIISI

Yndåle instructs her charges in the ways of strengthening their attractive ability, not only their personal attraction but also the attractiveness of their magical creations. This power is such a profound one that those born here are also shown how goodness and kindness increases beauty and how cruelty in time destroys one's attractiveness. Thus ethical concerns are attached to very practical effects and the process of karma, which is vital to the understanding of every elfin magician.

Therefore these elfin must learn in this lifetime the important balance between power and justice and the elven understanding that to be fair is to be fair.

October 5th

Arynthel: As Good as the Best

Magic: Horn of Calling
Constellation: Vanus, Volans
Planetary Association: Mercury
Faerie Assistants: Akka

The elfin born on this day seek excellence and the company of excellence, for this spirit demonstrates how using one's power as a means of rising above others limits one's spirit while using one's power to empower others empowers ones'elf. Therefore, these fae frequently seek the company of those who are their equals or who are better than they at the arts they seek to master for they desire, above all else, to improve thems'elves and their abilities.

There is often something eccentric or wild about these elves as they master this course of study, for they have given up trying to merely imitate others or follow tradition and now seek to create their own style and reimagine the traditional, in that way making all things their own.

> *A song constantly plays in the elven soul. Its melody is the call of adventure and its harmony is the call of Faerie.*

OCTOBER 6TH

Åbrethyn: A Light in the Darkness
MAGIC: HORN OF CALLING
CONSTELLATION: LARCA, LEO
PLANETARY ASSOCIATION: EARTH
FAERIE ASSISTANTS: DVERGAR

For those who have been struggling with the dark in their lives, these fae bring light and hope and a promise of a better tomorrow. In time, as they grow more adept, they take real action to help others toward the fulfillment of their better natures and their aspiration toward enlightenment. They are learning to *walk the talk*.

These elfin have often risen in the world overcoming darkness in their own lives and seek to help others do the same. They frequently work as counselors of some sort, or those who help the underprivileged, the abused or others who have simply made a wrong turn in life and now need a chance to redeem themselves.

OCTOBER 7TH

Leyndra: Blood Red Lips
MAGIC: SPEAR OF LIGHT AND DESTINY
CONSTELLATION: ROCHILA, PEGASUS
PLANETARY ASSOCIATION: NEPTUNE
FAERIE ASSISTANTS: LANDVÆTTIR

Leyndra teaches the positive use of passion and those born here come to learn the importance of fighting for what is right in the world. Thus these elfin often have an interest in the martial arts, the justice system, or fighting for the underdog. They are fervent and passionate both in the pursuit of what is right but also in their personal lives and relationships. They are frequently artists who use their art to awaken awareness in others.

October 8th
Vorfynre: Unique Perspective
Magic: Cauldron of Abundance, Cornucopia
Constellation: Gath, Crux
Planetary Association: Mars
Faerie Assistants: Di sma undar jordi

Vorfynre reveals the world and the dimensions from a new angle and those in his sphere of influence develop a fresh and unique way of looking at the world and what is going on around them. This often gives them insight in ways to success that others did not consider and they are sometimes inventors, researchers, or scientists exploring unusual or little considered areas of knowledge.

Thus these fae are often associated with ideas that transform the world and bring new insight to old ideas and are sometimes harbingers of the new and unexpected that the hidebound resist so fiercely.

October 9th
Tyndålys: Swordsmith
Magic: Sacred Pool
Constellation: Arandus, Reticulum
Planetary Association: Saturn
Faerie Assistants: Dökkálfar

This Shining One is especially the patron of the makers of magical "weapons", that is to say wands, staffs, canes, chalices, pentacles, robes, knives, swords, or other magical paraphernalia. This is a serious craft and this spirit reveals not only how to create such tools but also how to instill them with power. Those under his spirit's influence also learn how to cleanse tools previously owned by others, or how to take ordinary objects and transform them into magical talismans.

This path of instruction takes endurance and perseverance and thus those born here also learn these qualities as well as an attention to detail and an ability to concentrate on a spell without wavering.

October 10th

Rådåvyn: Run Through the Night Singing

Magic: The Stone of the Land
Constellation: Iranali, Pictor
Planetary Association: Earth
Faerie Assistants: Otso

This Shining One aids those who would create gatherings, covens, or fairy circles so that the energy of the land may be raised and we may unite with it for mutual benefit and success. All the practical aspects as well as the soulful and spiritual aspects of drawing together the kindred in a positive, exciting and memorable fashion will be revealed by this spirit to those in his care or those who seek his instruction and aid.

These elfin learn how to deal with a vast array of different personalities and how to get them to harmonize and work cooperatively. This instruction naturally carries over into their mundane lives in the world where they can experience great success if they utilize these lessons.

October 11th

Wevoryn: Wandering in Search Of

MAGIC: THE STONE OF THE LAND
CONSTELLATION: FOLI, LYRA
PLANETARY ASSOCIATION: PLUTO
FAERIE ASSISTANTS: ELDJÖTNAR

This place gives those born here a sense that there is something that they need to find or search for in order to make life complete. Sometimes, this prompts them to travel or move regularly, searching for the new. Sometimes, they spend their time in libraries or online exploring but ever they seek that missing piece to the puzzle and in doing so experience and discover many things they would not otherwise encounter and grow therefrom. In fact, they are usually not missing anything; that is just a carrot to urge them forward toward new experiences and enlightenment.

October 12th

Ufardyn: Rushes Over

MAGIC: STAFF OF POWER
CONSTELLATION: SETÅTRU, OPHIUCUS
PLANETARY ASSOCIATION: URANUS
FAERIE ASSISTANTS: FENODYREE

If you need help, these elfin will usually rush to assist you. This propensity can give some the idea that they are ever in a hurry or even desperate in some way, but really they just wish to be of aid. Under Ufardyn's guidance, they become more subtle in their manifestation and as they become adept their aid and guidance is much sought after and their arrival proclaimed with enthusiasm, for others know that the job will be done right and things will be put straight although their methods can be unusual, even shocking, to some. They make things anew.

October 13th

Rukorre: Senses the Possibilities

MAGIC: SHIELD OF LOVE AND PROTECTION
CONSTELLATION: ARAK, SAGITTARIUS
PLANETARY ASSOCIATION: MERCURY
FAERIE ASSISTANTS: FINFOLKAHEEM

Those under this spirit's aegis learn to see the world as energy lines and waves of power that they can follow or surf as they please. They learn the streams, rivers, roads and byways of energy that lead to whatever they desire, like a map of light laid out before them. It is seldom that these elfin get lost and if they do they can always instinctually find their way home again for they see things that are hidden from most folks and from this gain insight into the pathways into Faerie. If you are looking for the pathway, gateway or threshold, these adepts can point them out to you.

October 14th

Oledyn: Passion for Change

MAGIC: SACRED POOL
CONSTELLATION: ARELO, AURIGA
PLANETARY ASSOCIATION: EARTH
FAERIE ASSISTANTS: NÄKKI

When these elfin first begin on this course of life study, they may seem very traditional or resistant to change. In time, they come to seem restless and ever eager for the new, for that is what they are learning in this lifetime, to embrace the new, to delight in change, and to ever seek it. Thus these elfin can get bored easily although further evolution will show them the ways to keep thems'elves and others ever amused.

These individuals are learning the power of experience and as they do so they tend to hunger for more, for they come to understand that every new experience contributes to their knowledge and power.

October 15th

Maridyn: Misty Dawning

MAGIC: THE RINGS OF POWER
CONSTELLATION: GRADLI, TUCANA
PLANETARY ASSOCIATION: SATURN
FAERIE ASSISTANTS: MENNINKÄINEN

Maridyn reveals to these the first inklings of Faerie and the path thereto and although it may not be totally clear at first, somewhat a diluted taste, it none-the-less remains in their hearts and minds and serves as a beacon that ever calls them back again.

At the same time, these elfin often attempt to awaken others, and while they feel Faerie strongly within thems'elves sometimes have difficulty expressing it or explaining it adequately. They are counting on pure vibration to awaken others who as yet simply have not had that profound experience themselves. In time, they realize that each awakens in hir own time and these elfin learn to abide in strength and power awaiting those whose time has truly come.

> DESPITE WHAT STORIES SAY, ELVES DON'T TEND TO LIVE IN KINGDOMS OR QUEENDOMS BUT IN FREEDOMS.

OCTOBER 16ᵀᴴ

Jynher: Inches Near

MAGIC: THE RINGS OF POWER
CONSTELLATION: FAERO, TRIANGULUM
PLANETARY ASSOCIATION: MOON
FAERIE ASSISTANTS: FYLGJA

While it may seem at times to those born here that almost nothing of value happens in their life, and surely not quickly, they are making real spiritual and magical progress. It is just that this progress involves taking care of minute details, completing tasks left unfinished from previous lifetimes, and dealing with the minutia of the magical path. They sometimes hunger for excitement, and they sometimes get it as a stimulus to keep them going, but mostly they are here to develop the capacity to create intricate spells that only the truly adept can master and pull off successfully.

OCTOBER 17ᵀᴴ

Thedoryn: Starlight in a Raindrop

MAGIC: FAERY CIRCLE
CONSTELLATION: ILDRA, LEPUS
PLANETARY ASSOCIATION: VENUS
FAERIE ASSISTANTS: MOOINJER VEGGEY

These elfin are here to learn the wonder and magic of everyday life, to see starlight in a raindrop and the miraculous in the setting sun. As they grow increasingly adept at this, they are often seen as being a bit "off" by others, that is to say *off with the Faeries*, for they find joy where others perceive only drudgery and they encounter the mundane and other usually very boring aspects of the world with enthusiastic spirit. These adepts transform the world around them as they embrace all things with excitement.

October 18th
Tèleyn: Standing Near the Center
MAGIC: THE MAGIC MIRROR
CONSTELLATION: ROCHILA, PEGASUS
PLANETARY ASSOCIATION: ASTEROIDS
FAERIE ASSISTANTS: YSÄTTERS-KAJSA

Téleyn guides those under his tutelage to move to the calm center of the magic and from there shift and transform things with minimal effort and greatest effectivity. As these elfin develop they become increasingly aware of being in touch with and linked to the whole of life. As this sense of connection expands, so does their realm of influence.

To reach this level of development requires great maturity and one must truly feel connected in a positive way to all that is. This is not a function of authority but of loyal association.

October 19th
Diåfynle: Comfortable Among Them
MAGIC: CAULDRON OF REBIRTH
CONSTELLATION: ELPAN, CAMELOPARDALIS
PLANETARY ASSOCIATION: SATURN
FAERIE ASSISTANTS: JǫTUNN

The elfin born here are increasingly becoming comfortable and adapted to other dimensions, particularly the Faerie realms, and thus can enter those realms with increasing ease. Naturally, one can, as one often does, feel awkward at first in these new environments but with time and experience one is accepted as a part of the realm and embraced there.

Naturally, what realm one tends to wander into or explore depends on one's own proclivities, fate and destiny.

OCTOBER 20TH

Jåvere: Hovers Over

MAGIC: CAULDRON OF REBIRTH
CONSTELLATION: TONENYS, PUPPIS
PLANETARY ASSOCIATION: MERCURY
FAERIE ASSISTANTS: ISHIGAQ

This Shining One often deals with those who have awakened but are hesitant to proceed. The awakening is usually accompanied by a profound sense of wonder, rebirth and meaningfulness in one's life and one is naturally hesitant to yield these peak feelings to return to progressing slowly in the day to day world; but it is inevitable that one does this and this spirit shows those in her care how to do so while preserving that sense of magic within thems'elves.

These elfin learn to see the otherworldliness that resides along with the mundane and thus they transform their lives into a true faery tale.

IF SOMEONE REJECTS YOU, THANK THEM. THEY HAVE HELPED YOU MORE THAN YOU REALIZE.

—OLD ELVEN SAYING

The Silver Elves

OCTOBER 21ST
Oleda: Passionate Embrace

MAGIC: HORN OF CALLING
CONSTELLATION: KONALYMLE, HOROLOGIUM
PLANETARY ASSOCIATION: SUN
FAERIE ASSISTANTS: JÖRMUNGANDR

Oleda instructs her charges in the methods of embracing life, even grasping things that may seem negative or that one is less enthused about doing, and in this way transforming these things with the fae's own enthusiasm. This most often involves a psychological embrace more than a physical one, for one learns to accept individuals for who they are and as they present themselves, and in this way by accepting them, allow them to change. This is a very deep magic that only those who are adept understand.

At the same time, this Shining One can counsel those in her care on the use of water as an elemental power and particularly how to use this elemental avenue to enter the Faerie realms.

OCTOBER 22ND
Gylide: Fun to Have Around

MAGIC: CAULDRON OF REBIRTH
CONSTELLATION: ORMYN, CENTAURUS
PLANETARY ASSOCIATION: VENUS
FAERIE ASSISTANTS: BIEGGOLMAI

The elfin under this spirit's guidance have the opportunity, if they wish it, to develop their personalities so that they become magnetic, charismatic and powerful. As they become adept, people perceive them as being fun or a joy to be around and thus they are welcomed nearly everywhere and missed when they are gone.

Because of this, these elfin have a transformative effect on others who are willing and eager to accept their advice for they perceive that these fae have something very special about them and wish to be a part of it.

OCTOBER 23ᴿᴰ

Nådyndre: New Way of Doing Things

MAGIC: THE MAGIC MIRROR
CONSTELLATION: FROHAMËL, COMA BERENICES
PLANETARY ASSOCIATION: EARTH
FAERIE ASSISTANTS: FOSSEGRIMEN

These elfin are innovators, at least they are once this Shining One is done instructing them. They are ever experimenting with new ways of doing things, whether it be adapting recipes in cooking, or trying out new spells and formulas of magic. They may, but seldom do, invent the totally new, rather they tend to rework what already exists to make it better, more beautiful and successful.

Thus these elfin also, as they evolve and are increasingly adept, have the ability to remake the world. They are fix-it-upper people who take what may have been spoiled or discarded and give it new life.

> *THE SHINING ONES SAY THAT AT THE END OF THE UNIVERSE, WE WILL ALL TAKE A BOW. AND THE ELVES WILL THROW THE CAST PARTY!*

October 24th

Wivedyn: Want to Be There When It Happens

Magic: The Rings of Power
Constellation: Tonenys, Puppis
Planetary Association: Mercury
Faerie Assistants: Vittra

Wivedyn deals with those who are eager or ready to be in the center of the action. These elfin want to experience life fully and want to be a part of the scene, wherever it's happening, and thus follow the magic about seeking the places where it is flowering. Like volcanoes that change position from time to time, becoming dormant in one place while erupting in a new one, these fae ever seek that new eruption where Faerie is bursting forth into the world and under this spirit's care become ever more adept at finding it.

October 25th

Isynre: Hears Them Coming

Magic: Horn of Calling
Constellation: Nesnor, Norma
Planetary Association: Mercury
Faerie Assistants: Alfar

The elfin born here come to sense the approach of energy. They become attuned to power and they know instinctively those who have it and those that don't and they can feel when those with power, either positive or negative, approach and can stay or vacate the area as they deem best. Because of this ability, these elfin have a general sense of being protected, for they learn to be "not there" when trouble approaches. These fae become adept at finding energy spots/people and absorbing the free energy they radiate.

OCTOBER 26TH

Lidedyn: Love Shows the Way

MAGIC: STAFF OF POWER
CONSTELLATION: RAGOL, VIRGO
PLANETARY ASSOCIATION: ASTEROIDS
FAERIE ASSISTANTS: TJAETSIEÅLMAJ

Lidedyn teaches these elfin the power of love and how love is an energy that one can follow toward success, that is to say one can literally perceive it as a magical force, as one sees light, and use it as signposts toward fulfillment. Of course, to do this, one must surround one's s'elf with loving energy and people and to treat all others with kindness and respect, thus one becomes increasingly sensitive to its vibration and can spot its trail or jet stream anywhere it passes. Because of this, these fae transform their lives in deep and profound ways ever finding the best in every situation.

OCTOBER 27TH

Sijåndor: Sizzling Mood

MAGIC: THE RINGS OF POWER
CONSTELLATION: SABÅRWA, AQUARIUS
PLANETARY ASSOCIATION: JUPITER
FAERIE ASSISTANTS: ASKAFROA

These elfin learn to sizzle with magic. They don't have to say a word or do a thing but those around them sense there is something immense and powerful beneath their quiet exterior. They radiate and exude power and this, more often than not, attracts opportunity to them while deterring potential opposition.

The elfin born here tend to become extremely perceptive in their quiet way, absorbing energy without draining others, for they learn how to cycle the energy through them and out again, revitalizing all around them. Thus they are frequently students of Qigong and other energy working techniques.

October 28th

Glorynda: Forest Keeper

MAGIC: CAULDRON OF ABUNDANCE, CORNUCOPIA
CONSTELLATION: VANUS, VOLANS
PLANETARY ASSOCIATION: MARS
FAERIE ASSISTANTS: NØKKEN

Needless to say, these elfin usually love the trees and the forest and like to be as near to them as possible. At the same time, they come to understand that the entire world is a type of forest and even when they live in cities they find power in the trees that grow there. They also develop the ability to attune to the forest that was, thus even in cities they can draw forth the energy of the forests that once grew there, or will grow there in the future or that currently grow there in alternate dimensions. This is an advanced magic and these elfin must grow increasing adept to draw on this power.

> *MEN SAY LIFE IS AN ETERNAL STRUGGLE BETWEEN GOOD AND EVIL, WHEREAS ELVES SEE LIFE AS A CONTINUOUS STRUGGLE TO AWAKEN.*

OCTOBER 29TH

Charynde: Builds the Future

MAGIC: THE STONE OF THE LAND
CONSTELLATION: ROCHILA, PEGASUS
PLANETARY ASSOCIATION: MOON
FAERIE ASSISTANTS: LIEAIBOLMMAI

Charynde instructs those under her influence on the practical means of making Faerie real, that is come alive fully and manifest in the material world. These elfin learn to commune with and draw up the energy of the land wherever they abide and unite with its power in a sacred marriage of Earth and Stars bringing the Magical and the Mundane into harmony and deep and positive association.

These elfin learn the power of nurturing and often take on others as their magical charges and children, empowering and uplifting them. They become leaders in their community without any need of exoteric authority or titles.

OCTOBER 30TH

Umurde: The Company of Elves

MAGIC: FAERY CIRCLE
CONSTELLATION: ZILONA, URSA MAJOR
PLANETARY ASSOCIATION: URANUS
FAERIE ASSISTANTS: TROLLS

Umurde shows those under her care the means of creating truly elven communities, which is to say communities that are not only composed of elves but welcome all sincere individuals of every magical race. These communities are almost always artistic in nature, with painters, musicians, and writers, interwoven with Jack-of-all-trades Rangers and Gerry Rigging inventors.

While these communities often change, even disappear in time, they serve as an example of what is possible in the world and usually leave legends, sometimes myths, concerning them.

OCTOBER 31ST

Qefidyn: Remembers the Way

MAGIC: THE STONE OF THE LAND
CONSTELLATION: TARUNTUS, HYDRUS
PLANETARY ASSOCIATION: MERCURY
FAERIE ASSISTANTS: LEIB-OLMAI

The elfin born on this day awaken to a sense that the secrets to Faerie, and the secret ways to Faerie, exist within them and they just need to tap into their memories of previously lifetimes to access them. Naturally, these elfin attract others of our kind to them, for they increasingly develop the ability to speak of the magical realms and their past lives there and associate them with a vision of the future. They often speak of the Ancient Future, for they know that the world develops in cycles and what has been will come to be again in new ways.

> *THE SHINING ONES EVER WISH THE BEST FOR US AND THEY FULFILL THAT WISH BY HELPING US BECOME THE VERY BEST WE CAN BE.*

NOVEMBER

Mandrel: Making Sacred
Month: November
Magic: Apotheoturgy
Continent: Pacific Islands
Constellation: Elpan, Camelopardalis
Planetary Association: Mars
Faerie Assistants: Ka-poe-kino-pua

Mandrel is guardian of the spirits of November and teaches Apotheoturgy or Apotheosis, the magical art of making things or people sacred, thus he rules sacred springs, holy water and the waters of anointment. He guides those born or living in or descended from the peoples of the Pacific Islands. He can bring the dead back to life, or inspire the aged with youth so they feel and act young again. He moves one toward physical immortality.

Qidyndål: Draws Down the Magic
NOVEMBER 1ST TO 10TH
Magic: Huna
Area: Hawaiian Islands
Constellation: Ildra, Lepus
Planetary Association: Pluto
Faerie Assistants: Menehune

Qidyndål the Shining One is assisted by the Menehunes who are brownie, pixie, dwarf spirits of the Hawaiian Islands. He can teach one the magic of Huna and its associative Polynesian magics. He is also a great expert on the subject of the lost continent of Mu, of which Hawaii was a part, and on the third root race when genetic species had as yet not become fully formed so there were satyrs, centaurs and all manner of mixed species. He can also speak very wisely on the evolution of the animal species. He is related to Pluto and can help one understand how destruction is sometimes a significant part of the evolutionary path.

Gylefal: Fire of the Spirit
NOVEMBER 11TH TO 20TH

MAGIC: PYROTURGY

AREA: POLYNESIA AND SOMOA

CONSTELLATION: HOLVORO, FORNAX

PLANETARY ASSOCIATION: JUPITER

FAERIE ASSISTANTS: KAKAMORA

This Shining One is a master of Pyroturgy or the Magic of Fire. She is assisted by the Kakamora who are tree spirits related to pixies. She is a very benevolent spirit and will eagerly aid any who seek her assistance. Because of hir magic, she is associated with the Phoenix and the Fire Bird and can help the magician understand how fire, or stress and tension, can help one excel and she is the especial patron of those individuals who are attracted to high pressure and high intensity work and will teach them how to live in the fire so to speak like a salamander without getting burnt, in fact, she will show them how to thrive in this environment.

> MEN SAY YOU ONLY HAVE ONE LIFE TO LIVE. ELVES SAY YOU ONLY HAVE ONE LIFE TO LIVE AT A TIME.

Urynthal: Makes Manifest
NOVEMBER 21ST TO 30TH
MAGIC: CONJURY
AREA: ALEUTIAN ISLANDS, KAMCHATKA, KURIL ISLANDS
CONSTELLATION: SETÂTRU, OPHIUCUS
PLANETARY ASSOCIATION: URANUS
FAERIE ASSISTANTS: KORO-POK-GURU

Koro-pok-guru are the little people of the Ainu, who are related to the Faerie People of Europe, Ireland, Wales, Scotland and England (see Laurence Gardner *The Realm of the Ring Lords*) but are the aboriginal peoples of the northern islands of Japan and who lived there prior to the coming of the Japanese. These wee ones assist Urynthal in her efforts to teach conjury or the Art of Conjuring. She can show the magician how to take the simple and make it more beautiful, how to do much with little, making the most of everything within one's power, thus she will help the magician to maximize one's power in everyway. Her great wisdom will aid the elf to bring forth or conjure the latent powers and abilities in everyone the elf meets and to create opportunities where there previously seemed none available.

NOVEMBER 1ST
Diynfa: Connecting to the Magic
MAGIC: STAFF OF POWER
CONSTELLATION: ARANDUS, RETICULUM
PLANETARY ASSOCIATION: NEPTUNE
FAERIE ASSISTANTS: HANAU EPE

Diynfa teaches her students the means of connecting to the Magic, that is to say to the Source of All Things, All Power and All

Possibility. Those who learn this lesson need never be exhausted or run out of energy if they use this power well.

As one becomes adept here, one can shape the world as they desire and soon these fae will be creating their own realms and dimensions of being. But perhaps their greatest skill is their power to channel the energy and thus empower others, filling them with light and vibrant life.

November 2ⁿᵈ

Tikyndre: Steps into Sunshine

MAGIC: SWORD OF TRUTH AND JUSTICE
CONSTELLATION: ATAROLD, MONOCEROS
PLANETARY ASSOCIATION: JUPITER
FAERIE ASSISTANTS: AGLOOLIK

Those under this Shining One's care must make a determined decision to step into the light, that is pursue the positive in life or else follow the dark path of personal empowerment at the expense of others, or fall back into a wasted and depressing life in which they find thems'elves unable to decide at all.

Those who embrace this path become filled with energy and power and seize their path with determination. Once having decided, they can make fast progress and achieve much.

ELVES CONSIDER NATURE AS THE GREATEST SCIENTIST FOR IT IS EVER EXPERIMENTING.
—ANCIENT ELVEN KNOWLEDGE

NOVEMBER 3ᴿᴰ

Nejynde: Of the Stillness

MAGIC: CAULDRON OF REBIRTH
CONSTELLATION: ECH, HERCULES
PLANETARY ASSOCIATION: PLUTO
FAERIE ASSISTANTS: KAKAMORA

Often those born here have touched the core of the magic, the deep place of silence, contemplation and inner stillness, and now are emerging again, reshaping their lives and choosing new directions for thems'elves. Nejunde aids them to do this in the easiest fashion possible, awakening them gently into the world of awareness and possibility.

In many ways, these elfin are reawakening their physical, sensual s'elves, re-entering the world, having touched Spirit they now bring that spiritual energy back to the world, helping to renew it and fill it with magic once again.

NOVEMBER 4ᵀᴴ

Nymbar: Drawn to Starlight

MAGIC: THE MAGIC MIRROR
CONSTELLATION: PUTOR, SCULPTOR
PLANETARY ASSOCIATION: MOON
FAERIE ASSISTANTS: AMAROK

Some might think those born here are enamored of thems'elves, they may even stare for long periods in the mirror in seemingly narcissistic fascination, but really they are in wonder of thems'elves in a most innocent way. It is quite possible that some of these were not quite so attractive in previous lifetimes and now find thems'elves wondrous to look at. Others simply sense that there is something special about them and hope that by looking they will discover what it is. They are seeing the beginnings of their true s'elves emerging into the world, and that is a thing of wonder indeed. In time, they will get used to thems'elves and proceed merrily onward.

November 5th

Zelynde: Word Wise

MAGIC: FAERY CIRCLE
CONSTELLATION: URMA, DORADO
PLANETARY ASSOCIATION: NEPTUNE
FAERIE ASSISTANTS: HATUIBWARI

These elfin are introduced to the secret words and languages of faerie magic, become adept at using the various magical scripts for their spell casting and learn how to empower their words, even those they speak with on a day to day basis with power and vibrancy. They are on the way to becoming powerful practitioners of sorcery.

Because of this increasing power, these fae develop the ability to alter their fate and shift from one world situation to another for they easily learn the language of various realms and thus are well accepted and fit in with little effort.

> *THE ELVES BELIEVE ALL THE UNIVERSE IS DANCING.*

The Shining Ones

NOVEMBER 6TH

Widåve: Wanders in Search Of

MAGIC: THE STONE OF THE LAND
CONSTELLATION: LOWA, ERIDANUS
PLANETARY ASSOCIATION: SUN
FAERIE ASSISTANTS: KAHAUSIBWARE

These elfin are ready for a Quest and this spirit aids them to find the one that is appropriate for them, that is to say the one that is both challenging for their spiritual growth, possible to fulfill, but not too easy. This is a lifetime of challenges and those that embrace these lessons will progress swiftly and surely.

In a certain way, these elfin are learning to be accepting, that is accepting of the challenges laid before them and yet at the same time they are not docile individuals but rather, once set upon their path, quite active in pursuing it. They come to realize that every obstruction they confront will increase their knowledge, experience and power.

NOVEMBER 7TH

Tylynle: Swims Deep

MAGIC: CAULDRON OF REBIRTH
CONSTELLATION: TONENYS, PUPPIS
PLANETARY ASSOCIATION: EARTH
FAERIE ASSISTANTS: WENTSHUKUMISHITEU

While these elfin may have an affinity for water, their real love is usually the depth of the psyche. They want to know what makes thems'elves and others tick and often study psychology to help them understand. Their real course is, however, in the shamanic and sorcerous arts and sciences and they acquire the ability to help others get into and clear away the sediment of the past and to make thems'elves anew and reinvent thems'elves.

Because of the fact that they have cleared away their own inner baggage, and because they know they are able to help others as well, they become quite sure of thems'elves and very confident in their magic. They often make powerful exorcists.

November 8th

Nåmadyn: Noble Act

Magic: Horn of Calling
Constellation: Latur, Indus
Planetary Association: Jupiter
Faerie Assistants: Kamapua'a

Those born here frequently feel a need to redeem thems'elves or hope to advanced thems'elves through the noble deed or act, hoping in one vital movement to forge lifetimes ahead. In many ways, they sense that this event, this act will open the threshold for them and they will be able to step more directly into the realms of Faerie, into the dimensions of power. And they are not wrong. However, most often they must spend quite a bit of their life waiting for that moment to come, and if wise preparing.

November 9th

Zelizyn: Words Awaken

Magic: Staff of Power
Constellation: Urma, Dorado
Planetary Association: Pluto
Faerie Assistants: Elepaio

These elfin are particularly sensitive to words, their use, tone, and power and as adepts they become experts at using them. Thus these tend to get a great deal more from reading than most do. They can really read between the lines, or between the words, and are able to extrapolate a great deal that enhances their magic from the things they learn. They are able to take this inspiration and translate it into real visions that awaken others. As they progress, they are able to weave wisdom into their words and thus the most adept of these are often quoted.

November 10th

Årefyndre: Amused in Spite of Hirs'elf

Magic: Sacred Pool
Constellation: Coma, Aries
Planetary Association: Mercury
Faerie Assistants: Kapre

This Shining One teaches the art of humor, of realizing the amusing side of life and the circumstances one faces, and you may see these elfin quietly smiling or laughing at the shenanigans of the world. This is not intentional, really, they don't mean to make fun of people or laugh about what they do, but they just can't help thems'elves. The ironies of life become quite clear to them and they have finally gotten the cosmic joke.

Some might think that they feel superior to others, but really their humor is quite innocent, they are not laughing at people so much as with them. It's not their fault that others don't get the joke.

> *The Elves say that every star is the genius of the Magic unfolding.*

November 11th

Tridynfyr: Sudden Awareness

Magic: Cauldron of Abundance, Cornucopia
Constellation: Lacatar, Leo Minor
Planetary Association: Pluto
Faerie Assistants: Bariaua

These elfin are prone to sudden revelation and insight. These revelations may come as solutions to problems they've been facing or avenues to new opportunity they may wish to explore. At times, it is a deeper insight into things that they had previously assumed they had understood fully, only to find there is a doorway to new worlds in a room they thought did not have doors.

Thus as they advance these elfin develop the power of foresight and precognition and can see far into the future revealing possibilities for thems'elves and others. They are often seen as being far ahead of their time. These elfin often develop the power of prophecy.

November 12th

Fyryndor: Finding the Way Back

Magic: The Stone of the Land
Constellation: Setåtru, Ophiucus
Planetary Association: Mercury
Faerie Assistants: Aumakua

These fae usually carry within them a strong sense of their previous lifetimes in Faerie and feel that they are spending this life finding their way back, following that inner sense and memory to its source. At the same time, they feel attached to the land, and consequently often feel that they need to go or be in a particular

The Shining Ones

place, spot or country to find the portal home, often in the wilds of Nature, or the home of their ancestors.

In time, they begin to understand that the connection to Faerie can be heightened anywhere and they have the means of creating this powerful magic.

NOVEMBER 13TH
Håforvyn: Gradual Awakening
MAGIC: HORN OF CALLING
CONSTELLATION: KONALYMLE, HOROLOGIUM
PLANETARY ASSOCIATION: ASTEROIDS
FAERIE ASSISTANTS: XHUUYA

Unlike so many that are in a hurry to awaken their elven nature, this spirit teaches these fae how developing slowly is more enduring in the long run and more profound. Many who suddenly awaken to their elfin nature fall away in time attracted by this or that fad, but these determined fae carry on long after others, who had seemed at first to be so much further along than they, have given up.

Their steady approach becomes a source of strength for them and soon others are attracted to their steadfast pursuit of the Elven Way.

WHEN THE ELVES SAY THE UNIVERSE IS ONE, THEY DO NOT MEAN IT IS THE SAME BUT THAT IT IS ALL CONNECTED.

November 14th

Weforys: Waiting for the Sign
MAGIC: HORN OF CALLING
CONSTELLATION: FAERO, TRIANGULUM
PLANETARY ASSOCIATION: SUN
FAERIE ASSISTANTS: TAPAIRU

This Shining One helps the elfin born here to be ready for the sign that will come to them that will determine their course for lifetimes yet to come and let them know what their next quest will be. The exact nature of the quest, of course, depends upon the individual elfin spirit.

These fae have already accomplished something significant, and they have a sense of this although they don't usually remember the precise details of what they have done and others often look at them in this lifetime and wonder why these fae feel so proud of themselves when they have accomplished little that they can see or know of. But these elfin inwardly know, as do the Shining Ones, that they have advanced on the path of s'elf realization.

November 15th

Måkynsor: Masters the Technique
MAGIC: THE MAGIC MIRROR
CONSTELLATION: FOLI, LYRA
PLANETARY ASSOCIATION: NEPTUNE
FAERIE ASSISTANTS: WIKRAMADATTA

This spirit teaches those under his influence to master the particular magical techniques they've been studying. Depending on their level of development, this can be the mastery of the fundamentals to the mastery of the more esoteric and advanced techniques. This spirit also helps these elves see how once having mastered the techniques they can alter them, improve them and make them their own.

These elfin come to understand that they are part of a magical tradition and that they have just as much right to alter the techniques as those who originally created them. What matters always is how well they work.

NOVEMBER 16TH

Zomerys: Writes of Great Deeds

MAGIC: CAULDRON OF REBIRTH
CONSTELLATION: FAERO, TRIANGULUM
PLANETARY ASSOCIATION: URANUS
FAERIE ASSISTANTS: WALUTAHANGA

Zomerys draws those who are storytellers, writers, mythmakers, and raconteurs to him. Those born here are urged to develop their skills in these arts and this Shining One will do all in his power to aid them. Much will be revealed here, including how myths shape our thinking and our behavior and are in themselves a profound magical spell and can be used to awaken the spirit in others and connect them with the Collective Unconscious and the power of the ancestors.

This Shining One will also reveal how legends can arouse passion and spiritual or patriotic fervor, stir the souls of those who hear them and how this arousal is most powerful when felt by the speaker who evokes it.

> *WHAT DO ELVES SEEK IN THE WORLD? WE SEEK TO AWAKEN THE MAGIC IN ALL WE ENCOUNTER.*

NOVEMBER 17TH

Refidor: Secret to Success

MAGIC: THE STONE OF THE LAND
CONSTELLATION: GRADLI, TUCANA
PLANETARY ASSOCIATION: PLUTO
FAERIE ASSISTANTS: TIGMAMANUKAN

Refidor reveals the secrets to success to those in his care and as they come to comprehend these powerful spells they can obtain nearly anything they desire in the world. These elfin are learning how to make the land productive and our people prosperous and are vital powers in the quest to manifest Faerie.

Naturally, the temptation here is to use this power exclusively for personal advantage; however, Refidor will show these elfin how doing so would hinder the success they are attempting to achieve, that prosperity is greatest when shared, and the more one invests wisely the greater will be the return.

NOVEMBER 18TH

Nanara: Not Afraid to Reveal the Truth

MAGIC: SACRED POOL
CONSTELLATION: PIHYR, SEXTANS
PLANETARY ASSOCIATION: SATURN
FAERIE ASSISTANTS: DEGEI

These elfin, under this spirit's instruction, are learning to tell the truth in such a way as it will be more readily received. These are often fearless fae who in previous lifetimes have been whistleblowers who spoke truth to power or to the people about those in power but who have a tendency to be inordinately blunt and thus often offend when they mean only to help. Nanara shows them the importance of considering other's feelings when delivering the truth and ways of doing so that make the painful revelation more acceptable.

November 19th

Boryndal: Bends with the Time

MAGIC: THE STONE OF THE LAND
CONSTELLATION: ATAROLD, MONOCEROS
PLANETARY ASSOCIATION: EARTH
FAERIE ASSISTANTS: TIZHERUK

These elfin are learning how to adapt their magic to the times and the circumstances they are living within. They become deeply attuned to the land and the spirits that abide there and thus consequently are making offerings to the spirits of a particular area, making allies among the flora, fauna, and invisible spirits of the region where they live or visit. Thus wherever they go they have allies in the spirit world and great luck is the result.

It takes time to connect to the secret pathways in an area. For some it may take years for them to get to know the best places to eat, buy things, or connect to others of their kind, but with this spirit's aid all this happens more quickly and easily for those he teaches.

> *SCIENCE IS THE METHOD; KNOWLEDGE IS THE KEY; LOVE IS THE PATH; AND MAGIC IS THERE RESULT.*

NOVEMBER 20TH

Zigorys: World of Wonder
MAGIC: STAFF OF POWER
CONSTELLATION: COMA, ARIES
PLANETARY ASSOCIATION: MARS
FAERIE ASSISTANTS: NAITAKA

These budding Thaumaturgists or wonder workers are becoming powerful indeed and this Shining One can show them how to use their power to greatest effect, awakening the imaginations and inner spirit of others. Sometimes these enchanters disguise thems'elves as stage magicians or illusionists and like these performers reveal the secrets of their art only to the initiated.

They tend to attract loyal followers and assistants who sense that these fae have some secrets powers that they hope to absorb by vibrational proximity and they are indeed correct and will thems'elves most likely come under this spirit's tutelage in the future.

NOVEMBER 21ST

Holaryn: Great Opportunity
MAGIC: THE RINGS OF POWER
CONSTELLATION: ARANDUS, RETICULUM
PLANETARY ASSOCIATION: MARS
FAERIE ASSISTANTS: ENGKANTO

Those born under this spirit's influence will have a great opportunity to pass into the deeper realms of esoteric knowledge in this lifetime, to pass one of the Rings Pass Not, and thus be initiated into a higher level of adeptship. In other words, they will have a chance to graduate with the attendant privileges, powers and rights thereof. This means greater and more intimate contact with the Shining Ones and more responsibility in coming lifetimes.

NOVEMBER 22ND

Duarys: Dedicated to the Cause

MAGIC: CAULDRON OF ABUNDANCE, CORNUCOPIA
CONSTELLATION: HOLVORO, FORNAX
PLANETARY ASSOCIATION: MERCURY
FAERIE ASSISTANTS: DAMA DAGENDA

These elfin, once they have truly awakened, tend to dedicate their lives to the cause of manifesting Faerie and will give all that they have to that cause, not only their wealth, but more importantly their life devotion. Until they awaken they often have various worldly interests and obsessions that hold their attention, but these are but a substitute for that higher spiritual devotion to which they will eventually awaken. To others, these fae often seem a bit wild or crazy, so absorbed are they in their interests, but they, for their part, couldn't care less about what others think.

NOVEMBER 23RD

Hilale: Good with Children

MAGIC: FAERY CIRCLE
CONSTELLATION: ARAK, SAGITTARIUS
PLANETARY ASSOCIATION: MARS
FAERIE ASSISTANTS: CAMPHURCII

These fae are naturally good with children and make good parents, teachers, and guides of the young. Some write children's books, and others simply have a facility to be a child among children, easily accepted by them, and understanding them perfectly. Thus they make good therapists for children. Curiously, some of them never have children of their own but adopt every child as a subject of their magic and their care. They are quite active elfin and know how to get down on the floor and play.

NOVEMBER 24TH

Evarfyn: Elf Wizard
MAGIC: SACRED POOL
CONSTELLATION: FADRON, PERSEUS
PLANETARY ASSOCIATION: PLUTO
FAERIE ASSISTANTS: SANTELMO

This Shining One is an instructor in elf wizard academy and those born here have been invited to attend. They can refuse if they wish, of course, but will nonetheless have a tendency to develop one or more special skills and abilities and will often be seen as highly advanced and talented individuals.

Those who embrace this course of study will be offered all the mini-courses that come with wizardry, which includes both the s'elf confidence to work alone, and the devotion to strive for the general wellbeing as well as the particular magics that are their especial interest.

NOVEMBER 25TH

Foneda: Feeling Satisfied
MAGIC: STAFF OF POWER
CONSTELLATION: SALMO, PISCES AUSTRINUS
PLANETARY ASSOCIATION: VENUS
FAERIE ASSISTANTS: PUNTAN

These elfin have the opportunity to learn the power of satisfaction, of being satisfied within thems'elves but also of bringing satisfaction to others and the rewards that are accrued thereby. Make no mistake, this is a truly great power, although one must be alert and vigilant and not fall into indolence and conceit if one is to use it successful and not arouse needless opposition.

This spirit teaches these fae how to radiate this energy in a modest but powerful way so it not only attracts others to them, but also transforms the environments they inhabit. As long as they can remain modest and avoid arrogance, this power will serve them well.

November 26th

Refadyn: Secret Way

MAGIC: HORN OF CALLING
CONSTELLATION: FROHAMĖL, COMA BERENICES
PLANETARY ASSOCIATION: JUPITER
FAERIE ASSISTANTS: SKOOKUM

Refadyn gives special instruction to those born here in the secret ways that pertain to their individual path, how to attract or find those who are kin to them, and how to get the most from association with others who are on a similar path. The particular secrets revealed will depend on the individual, their level of development and their chosen course of study.

Also, if there are any areas these elfin are weak in, this spirit will help them improve thems'elves in these studies and show them tricks that will make these subjects more interesting and much easier for them to learn, so instead of avoiding them they will embrace these topics with relish.

November 27th

Syrynta: Distant Shores
Magic: Cauldron of Abundance, Cornucopia
Constellation: Sacro, Crater
Planetary Association: Venus
Faerie Assistants: Pinari

These are often perceived of as *the grass is always greener on the other side* people for they have a sense that there is a better world than this and that one can with time and effort find it. This spirit helps them to understand that it is their duty to create this better world in their own lives and in this way make it real or manifest in the world at large. These individuals often have an innate sense of the good and the beautiful and in time strive to create it in all that they do. Thus, as they become increasingly adept, they become true examples for others to model their lives upon.

November 28th

Wefynfe: Waits for the Right Moment
Magic: Horn of Calling
Constellation: Raltosor, Corona Australis
Planetary Association: Venus
Faerie Assistants: Haietlik

Wefynfe teaches the art of timing, especially in relationship, of waiting for the right moment to act, speak, inquire, approach or retreat. This is a very important magical technique that has important uses in even the simple exchanges people encounter on a daily basis. Of course, this small understand of timing, leads to the comprehension of timing on a larger scale and this course is just the beginning or refinement of other courses of study.

These elfin know when to help, when to hold back, and when to mind their own business. They come to understand how much they can aid someone without rendering them powerless or bringing them harm by doing so. They ever seek to inspire, empower and help.

NOVEMBER 29ᵀᴴ

Zormarfyn: Wizard's Ways

MAGIC: THE STONE OF THE LAND
CONSTELLATION: RIFRO, PHOENIX
PLANETARY ASSOCIATION: NEPTUNE
FAERIE ASSISTANTS: NEVINBIMBAAU

Zormarfyn teaches the secrets of Wizardry and the ways to use wizardry to obtain power and success in everyday life. Essentially, she teaches hedge-wizardry or the art of making the practical and mundane, magical. These elfin learn to draw energy from the land and circulate it about increasing the vibrancy of the area they inhabit. They also learn the secret ley lines and avenues of power, and how the world also has its lines of power through electrical connections, satellite and radio waves and how all these can be made to serve one's spells.

NOVEMBER 30ᵀᴴ

Farmiyn: Every Bit Counts

MAGIC: SPEAR OF LIGHT AND DESTINY
CONSTELLATION: ARANDUS, RETICULUM
PLANETARY ASSOCIATION: SATURN
FAERIE ASSISTANTS: HUAKA'I PŌ

You might call these the *waste not want not folks*, for these elfin learn the art of using everything and utilizing the power of everyone, discarding and discounting none, for success. These fae are becoming magi and with increasing adeptship attract their own students and carry on their own courses of study.

But most of all these elfin learn that even the smallest bit of energy, if used wisely, can produce magical effects and thus they learn to make the most of everything they have.

Evolution is like a relay race, we carry the baton of wisdom, power, and knowledge to those awaiting us in the future.

—Ancient Elven Knowledge

The Shining Ones say the fact that many people lie to make themselves seem better than they are reveals their inner hunger to evolve.

DECEMBER

ÈLAVYNDRÈL: TEACHES THE SECRETS

MONTH: DECEMBER

MAGIC: WIZARDRY

CONTINENT: ANTARCTICA, ALSO THE LOST CONTINENTS OF ATLANTIS, MU AND LEMURIA.

CONSTELLATION: ERTOR, MUSCA

PLANETARY ASSOCIATION: EARTH

FAERIE ASSISTANTS: OUROBOROS, SNAKE PEOPLE AND DRAGONS

Èlavyndrèl is assisted by the Snake and Dragon spirits and has influence over all the previous root races of humanity and those directly descended from them. Anyone who works in Antarctica comes under her influence. She rules wizardry and all those who do research. She is the inspirer of inventors of all sorts and those who take the old and refashion it in a new and better form. She thus also promotes recycling and rules the process of reincarnation.

THE ELVES BELIEVE THAT THE UNIVERSE BREATHES STARLIGHT AND WE ARE THAT BREATH.

Hylåval: Deep in the Tomes
DECEMBER 1ST TO 10TH
MAGIC: BIBLIOTURGY
AREA: ANTARCTICA
CONSTELLATION: DEOSA, CANCER
PLANETARY ASSOCIATION: SATURN
FAERIE ASSISTANTS: BARBEGAZI

Hylåval is the patron of librarians, bookstore owners and workers, particularly those who have metaphysical, esoteric and occult bookstores. She is aided by the Barbegazi, who are dwarf-gnome like beings. She is also the patron of sand-painters, that is those who use colored sand to create mandalas and other spiritual symbols. She teaches reflection, meditation and is associated with winter and the solemn considerations that often occur at that time.

Halåleal: Charts One's Destiny
DECEMBER 11TH TO 20TH
MAGIC: ASTROLOGY
AREA: ATLANTIS
CONSTELLATION: ERTOR, MUSCA
PLANETARY ASSOCIATION: JUPITER
FAERIE ASSISTANTS: TECUMBALAM

Halåleal is the Master of Astrology and is assisted by the Tecumbalam, the great birds of Mayan mythology. Halåleal can inform one about the second root race, those luminous gelatinous beings that were physical in the sense that pudding is physical. He is the patron of initiation and baptism and will anoint one toward one's true destiny as he sees with clarity the abilities, opportunities and obstructions that one can use or that one faces in their coming life from birth onward. He can help one understand how one's

The Shining Ones

natal chart does not define one but is rather a map concerning one's path in a particular life.

Myvaral: Blends the Elements
DECEMBER 21ST TO 31ST
MAGIC: ALCHEMY
AREA: MU AND LEMURIA
CONSTELLATION: JUFI, OCTANS
PLANETARY ASSOCIATION: MERCURY
FAERIE ASSISTANTS: TAOTAO MONA

This Shining One is the Master of Alchemy and with the aid of the Taotao Mona, or great ancestors, can teach one much in regard to this ancient and secret art. She can also tell one of the first root race, those beings of light who were only physical in the sense that fire is physical, and of its progress toward manifestation. She is a quite playful spirit and will help one understand the transitory or temporary nature of manifestation in the world and how our ultimate destiny is to return to this more ephemeral state of being. She can teach one much about using the body as a tool and how valuable it is for learning the lessons needed for manifesting all we will in the Universe.

DECEMBER 1ST
Refynthel: Secret Glances
MAGIC: SWORD OF TRUTH AND JUSTICE
CONSTELLATION: OLÉLTRE, TELESCOPIUM
PLANETARY ASSOCIATION: JUPITER
FAERIE ASSISTANTS: LAMASSU

Refynthel instructs those under her influence about all things regarding secret glances, the power of the eyes, the evil eye and how to protect ones'elf from it, micro-expressions and many other secrets. Thus these elfin sometimes study Neuro-linguistic programing and other arts that deal with universal expressions, eye movements and other aspects of human behavior.

Some might mimic these expressions as a means of deceiving others, actors may use them to convey a particular character accurately, but most of all these elfin are seeking the truth that lies beneath the surface in every situation.

December 2nd

Ovynve: Powerful Energy

MAGIC: STAFF OF POWER
CONSTELLATION: ELFASA, DELPHINUS
PLANETARY ASSOCIATION: NEPTUNE
FAERIE ASSISTANTS: AEGLE

This spirit teaches the elfin born here how to raise energy, especially their personal energy, how to increase their energy, and how to direct it in a focused fashion. She also knows everything worth knowing about the 4th root race, called the Atlanteans, and will instruct those in her care how one may gain greater understanding of this race by observing the behavior of teenagers.

Naturally, these elfin become quite powerful and this Shining One will help them understand how to use this energy in a potent way without engaging in endless conflicts, competition and juggling for position that ultimately only wastes one's time and effort.

THE ELVES SAY: "EVEN THE MYTHS EVOLVE!"

DECEMBER 3ᴿᴰ
Jireyn: I Live Among Them
MAGIC: THE STONE OF THE LAND
CONSTELLATION: ULOS, TAURUS
PLANETARY ASSOCIATION: SUN
FAERIE ASSISTANTS: WILL-O'-THE-WISP

These elfin are learning how to live successfully among others. They are perpetually "strangers in a strange land" (*I Ching*, Wilhelm, Baynes) and as they become adept can make friends anywhere and find positive reception in nearly any social environment. These fae learn that mere words, while potent, are not as powerful as emotive expression, and they learn to create thought emotes, that is to say words that touch the inner feelings of others and move them in powerful ways. They are also trained in the elfin magical arts of courtesy that ease their way through the world and heightens their possibilities of success.

DECEMBER 4ᵀᴴ
Häldor: Gets Things Moving
MAGIC: STAFF OF POWER
CONSTELLATION: PYKTAR, SAGITTA
PLANETARY ASSOCIATION: VENUS
FAERIE ASSISTANTS: APKALLU

This Shining One initiates activators, those that will get things going in any situation, and who can inspire and empower others. These elfin become leaders in the true sense, that is to say they start things, are always in the forefront, and are pioneers in their chosen fields of study and interest.

These elfin develop the ability to see possibilities that others do not and in many ways are doorway creators. They are not looking for the gateways to Faerie, they are in the process of creating them.

December 5th

Ändera: Always With Us

Magic: Shield of Love and Protection
Constellation: Focida, Chamaleon
Planetary Association: Uranus
Faerie Assistants: Crinaeae

Ändera helps those elfin who feel uncertain in their connection to Faerie and the Shining Ones, who have suffered and thus have doubts, how to regain their faith and to make it strong and powerful so that they know with certainty that everything happens for the best and they are always under the protection of the aura of Faerie.

These elfin are renewing their contact with the ancestors and with their ancient family of the faerie folk and this spirit will aid them with this so they will in time feel ever surrounded and embraced by the love of their elfin kin.

December 6th

Odoryn: Panther On a Rock

Magic: Sacred Pool
Constellation: Verpa, Hydra
Planetary Association: Sun
Faerie Assistants: Fire Elementals

These fae are learning how to store up power so it becomes great through accumulation and can be used for important things. This spirit will also instruct these elfin how to develop habits that lead to this accumulation, how to recognize what is significant and worth using their magic upon, and how to use magic on a daily basis without depleting one's s'elf or one's energy.

In the course of evolution these become very energetic and powerful wizards and magic wielders and become a source of nurturing energy for others in their care.

December 7th

Råvynthe: Sea Singer

Magic: The Rings of Power
Constellation: Lutra, Pisces
Planetary Association: Neptune
Faerie Assistants: Jievaras

These elfin are especially attuned to the sea and sea magic in all its forms, which means they have an association with the individual and collective unconsciousness, as well as the evolution of the human race through the third root race where humans first began to become clearly male or female and where there were for a time, satyrs, centaurs and other mixed race beings prior to increasing genetic selectivity. All of these matters and how this knowledge can be used to increase one's magical potency will be revealed by this Shining One to those in her care.

One elf is a torch. Two a beacon light. Three do make a circle and four the dance begins.

December 8th

Nyndra: Out of the Blue

Magic: Shield of Love and Protection
Constellation: Elpan, Camelopardalis
Planetary Association: Uranus
Faerie Assistants: Pegaeae

Nyndra teaches both the art of preparing for the unexpected, which is to say to always be prepared as much as possible for every eventuality, but also how to use the art of surprise to gain success. These elfin learn how to transition through difficult periods with the least stress and how to accept gracefully those things over which they have no power as yet, learning to trust in the guidance and protection of the Shining Ones and their elven kindred. As they become ever more adept, there is little that surprises these fae.

December 9th

Irynde: Heals with Herbs

Magic: Faery Circle
Constellation: Verpa, Hydra
Planetary Association: Mars
Faerie Assistants: Ghillie Dhu

These elfin are often becoming master herbalists but can also use their talents in the pharmaceutical industry (although they tend toward more natural modes of healing), in cooking, healing, chemistry or anything else involving herbs. Sometimes they are gardeners and grow the herbs of healing and enlightenment. These elfin also understand the importance of crop rotation, of infusing the soil with nutrients and other secrets for growing potent plants and herbs.

DECEMBER 10TH
Bërenyn: Beckons Us to Join
MAGIC: HORN OF CALLING
CONSTELLATION: ECH, HERCULES
PLANETARY ASSOCIATION: EARTH
FAERIE ASSISTANTS: JACULUS

This Shining One teaches the art of receptivity, of openness to others, and the ways to attract others and make them feel comfortable in one's presence. These elfin are evolving into gatherers who organize groups, clans, and gatherings, and who help others coordinate their efforts to optimize their success. These fae are networkers, web weavers and are forever inviting others to join in, come along and be part of the family. They know the magic of making people feel at home among them and are thus frequently found surrounded by others eager to assist them. Those who are just beginning the course of study are often still working out their issues in group association and are sometimes thrust into groups by the Shining Ones, such as the military or in schools, to aid them in this process. As they become increasingly adept, they see the many benefits of group association and are seldom found without their devoted others.

DECEMBER 11TH
Jemynlor: I Am the One
MAGIC: SPEAR OF LIGHT AND DESTINY
CONSTELLATION: SETÂTRU, OPHIUCUS
PLANETARY ASSOCIATION: SATURN
FAERIE ASSISTANTS: WATER ELEMENTALS

These fae are under this spirit's care to gain a sense of their own uniqueness, their specialness, but also to appreciate the unique and special nature of others. They are developing into eccentrics, thus elfin, and when adept will be singularities who are the birth seed of new ways of being.

In that sense, these elfin are often seen as messengers of the future, as far ahead of their time, and they offer alternative modes of being that detour from the norm and lead those who are inspired by their example deeper into Faerie.

DECEMBER 12TH

Vytoryn: Very Much So

MAGIC: HORN OF CALLING
CONSTELLATION: LANU, ARA
PLANETARY ASSOCIATION: SUN
FAERIE ASSISTANTS: HELEAD

These fae are learning to be prime exemplars of their chosen magical arts or of their sub-race of the faerie race. Some you may look at and say, they may be elfin or not, others you may see will bring Faerie strongly to your mind, but these will in time scream out with every aspect of their being that they are magical folk and there is simply no doubt about it.

The power of water and relationship is theirs and while they need not say a word they call out to the hearts and imaginations of those who are kindred to them, inspiring and empowering others just by passing by.

MEN SOMETIMES SAY THAT TIME IS OF THE ESSENCE. WE ELVES SAY THAT LOVE IS THE ESSENCE AND TIME THE MEANS OF MANIFESTING IT.

The Shining Ones

DECEMBER 13TH

Synfar: Song of Awakening

MAGIC: THE MAGIC MIRROR
CONSTELLATION: WYTRE, LIBRA
PLANETARY ASSOCIATION: MOON
FAERIE ASSISTANTS: NYKŠTUKAS

Synfar shows those under his guidance the means of touching the souls of others, of reaching into their spiritual depths and awakening their most primal wishes and aspirations. This creates a sense of simpatico; others feel that these fae really *get* them and thus this is a most profound power.

Naturally, as these elfin mature in this power they become increasingly sure of thems'elves, particularly in relationship to others, and thus must be cautious to use this power ethically or suffer the karma that attaches to its abuse.

DECEMBER 14TH

Zåvyntre: Wondrously Bright

MAGIC: THE STONE OF THE LAND
CONSTELLATION: SYRJAE, BOOTES
PLANETARY ASSOCIATION: PLUTO
FAERIE ASSISTANTS: KARZEŁEK

This Shining One instructs her charges on the means of illuminating the world by heightening their individual aura and in time these elfin literally glow. Among the many secrets that are revealed here are those concerning how individuals in love radiate energy and how pregnant women are quite often glowing, as well as the radiance of some children, and how to evoke this power within ones'elf.

Abundance tends to follow these fae who, in radiating light into the world, are also literally emanating magic, power, and success to those open enough to absorb it. They become a blessing to all who encounter them.

December 15th

Pikalyn: Rainbow Rising

MAGIC: FAERY CIRCLE
CONSTELLATION: NESNOR, NORMA
PLANETARY ASSOCIATION: MARS
FAERIE ASSISTANTS: JIEVARAS

Those born here are learning the power of diversity and how to bring various personalities into harmonious union. They may be match-makers of various sorts, for they develop the tendency to bring the right people together for romance or work or creative projects and know who is a good fit with someone else or for a particular situation.

Most of what they do is instinctual, rather than logical, and they easily go beyond what is said to them, or written on a page, to what lays in potential beneath it. They have an ability to work in human resources or even arbitration.

December 16th

Lofarfyn: Loves the Blade

MAGIC: CAULDRON OF ABUNDANCE, CORNUCOPIA
CONSTELLATION: RAGOL, VIRGO
PLANETARY ASSOCIATION: PLUTO
FAERIE ASSISTANTS: KUPOLĖ

Lofarfyn is a master martial artist and will aid anyone interested in understanding the mystical aspects of the fighting arts, sort of Zen and the Art of Kicking Someone's Ass. Most of all, this Shining One teaches those in her care how to win without engaging in conflict at all, the subtle arts of bluff, misdirection, redirection and yielding.

These elfin are usually protectors of the Earth and the flora and fauna on it. They protect the innocent and the abused and thus are often rewarded generously by those they have helped.

DECEMBER 17TH
Zargor: Wizard's Curiosity

MAGIC: SACRED POOL
CONSTELLATION: JANEL, GRUS
PLANETARY ASSOCIATION: URANUS
FAERIE ASSISTANTS: KIKIMORA

Zargor teaches the art of curiosity, of asking questions, of seeking to understand what is beyond and behind the patent answers and explanations that are typically given to and accepted by the masses.

Obviously, psychology can be of interest to these elfin, but also quantum physics, astronomy, nuclear physics and other sciences that seek to understand the beginnings of things, and the underlying and often invisible powers that move the world. They don't just want to know the techniques of magic; they want to know the underlying mechanics that make them work.

> *WHEN TWO OR MORE ARE GATHERED IN THE NAME OF FAERIE, SOMETHING WONDROUS IS BOUND TO OCCUR.*

December 18th

Emeråvyn: Chooses the Light

Magic: Faery Circle
Constellation: Deosa, Cancer
Planetary Association: Jupiter
Faerie Assistants: Gancanagh

This Shining One teaches the art of positive romance and relationship. How to overcome jealousy in ones'elf, how to help others rise above their envy and jealousy, and how to help those who are together to live in greater harmony and those who are separated how to treat each other with mutual respect.

Thus as these elfin advance on this course of study, they are often seem as being both very attractive but also very wise and others come to seek their counsel, particularly when it concerns love and romance.

December 19th

Gånfidèl: Fleet in Response

Magic: Cauldron of Rebirth
Constellation: Ifol, Lynx
Planetary Association: Venus
Faerie Assistants: Pucks

Gånfidèl instructs those born here how to make quick changes, how to embrace transformation, and how to reinvent thems'elves whenever they desire or they find it beneficial to do so. Thus these fae are learning the underlying arts of shapeshifting and can fit into any situation with ease.

These elfin are also quick to help, quick to restore things that have been damaged, and quick to help others start anew. When adept they make all things they touch better, improving all that they encounter.

December 20th

Jynvynve: Inner Calling

MAGIC: STAFF OF POWER
CONSTELLATION: ECH, HERCULES
PLANETARY ASSOCIATION: MARS
FAERIE ASSISTANTS: FOMOIRE

Jynvynve teaches the art of developing one's inner power, especially coming to understand one's true destiny and direction in and through the lifetimes. These elfin feel a calling but it is the calling of their own spirit urging them to become the perfected and powerful elfin they inwardly know thems'elves to be.

This sense of destiny becomes a deep inner passion for them that they can then redirect into the world to find the experiences, adventures, quests and studies that will help them achieve their true goals.

December 21st

Murfin: Natural Grace

MAGIC: SHIELD OF LOVE AND PROTECTION
CONSTELLATION: NALON, CORVUS
PLANETARY ASSOCIATION: VENUS
FAERIE ASSISTANTS: JAVINĖ

With this spirit's help the elfin born here are learning the basics of grace, of elegance, and of learning to be comfortable in their own bodies. In time, as they become more adept, this grace seems and becomes very natural, as though they were born with it, but in fact it has usually taken a concerned effort to integrate and coordinate the elements of their being and body with inner confidence and calm that has evolved into the ease of expression they come to manifest.

This grace of being extends to every aspect of their lives in time and can be applied to any art or activity they pursue.

December 22nd

Gradorn: Friend of the Lost
MAGIC: SHIELD OF LOVE AND PROTECTION
CONSTELLATION: LATUR, INDUS
PLANETARY ASSOCIATION: MARS
FAERIE ASSISTANTS: EARTH ELEMENTALS

Often these elfin have been lost in this or previous lifetimes and now under this spirit's guidance are learning to help other lost souls and spirits to find their way back to their true s'elves and their faerie natures, which means back to their inner and intimate connection to Faerie.

These fae frequently become lore keepers, who are able to use the ancient legends to awaken the elfin energy in others who are naturally aroused by this touch of Ancient Faerie. They are thus very active protectors of our legends and history.

EVIL MAGIC IS ULTIMATELY AN OXYMORON, FOR EVIL DESTROYS THE ECSTASY THAT ALL TRUE MAGIC DEPENDS UPON.

DECEMBER 23ʳᴰ

Vemarys: True to the Way

MAGIC: THE MAGIC MIRROR
CONSTELLATION: NERON, MENSA
PLANETARY ASSOCIATION: SATURN
FAERIE ASSISTANTS: KABOUTER

Vemarys helps those born under her influence to distinguish those things that are truly of Faerie and those that are merely the musings of writers who have yet to really connect to their elven nature, or who are still affected by the cultures of man and confuse these with our own true culture.

These elfin learn how to be true to their own s'elves and how to use their primal innocence as a guide to what is genuine and what is false. These elfin in time become very dedicated and serious practitioners of the Elven Way.

DECEMBER 24ᵀᴴ

Hůldyn: Great Personality

MAGIC: CAULDRON OF REBIRTH
CONSTELLATION: ÅNLEA, ANTLIA
PLANETARY ASSOCIATION: MOON
FAERIE ASSISTANTS: AQRABUAMELU

When these elfin are finished with this course of evolutionary study, they become very charismatic beings with incredible personalities and profound powers of persuasion. Some just starting here may seem reserved, introverted or even rather dull. Once they are adept, however, their mere presence will cause excitement. This does not mean they will no longer be introverts, if that is their inclination, but that as introverts they will radiate an aura of wisdom, mystery and profound knowledge that will touch others to their core.

DECEMBER 25TH

Soreryn: Snow Walker

MAGIC: SHIELD OF LOVE AND PROTECTION
CONSTELLATION: GATH, CRUX
PLANETARY ASSOCIATION: MARS
FAERIE ASSISTANTS: TYLWYTH TEG

Those born here are often subject to limiting financial circumstances and are learning how to make the most of little. These elfin become quite adept at being efficient. The expression *waste not, want not* is key to their evolution. Some of these have been spendthrifts in previous lifetimes and this course is a karmic lesson for them, others are preparing to initiate new realms with limited resources and wish to know how to do this successfully. In time, they all, if they pursue these lessons with devotion and determined effort, become very successful.

DECEMBER 26TH

Triyndre: Summoned by the Shining Ones

MAGIC: THE MAGIC MIRROR
CONSTELLATION: PUTOR, SCULPTOR
PLANETARY ASSOCIATION: PLUTO
FAERIE ASSISTANTS: FIR BOLG

These elfin feel the Call of the Shining Ones and know that there is a quest for them to fulfill in this lifetime. They also know that this spirit is preparing them for advancement in the evolutionary hierarchy and that they are truly moving up in the realms and dimensions of spiritual power. They are truly becoming otherworldly in a literal sense and will be evolving even greater eldritch power. However, this often means that others sense that there is something strange or unusual about these fae and these others usually treat them with caution.

DECEMBER 27ᵀᴴ

Gimaryn: For the First Time Ever

MAGIC: THE STONE OF THE LAND
CONSTELLATION: ECH, HERCULES
PLANETARY ASSOCIATION: MARS
FAERIE ASSISTANTS: EŽERINIS

These elfin are being introduced to new realms of understanding and experience in this lifetime and like a small child in a new world may react with wonder, uncertainty or wild enthusiasm depending on their soulful predisposition. They are especially learning all about the use of familiars, of allies among the wild creatures and the use of totems to invoke the primal powers of their animal s'elf. They also come to see their own progress through the lifetimes, their development in the animal realm in particular and their future among the Shining Ones.

DECEMBER 28ᵀᴴ

Brynfar: Blood Red Jewel

MAGIC: SPEAR OF LIGHT AND DESTINY
CONSTELLATION: URMA, DORADO
PLANETARY ASSOCIATION: EARTH
FAERIE ASSISTANTS: KOBOLDS

Brynfar teaches the art of drawing and channeling energy through jewels and crystals as well as the means of succeeding in the world in the diamond or other jewel related industries. This spirit also has influence over miners, prospectors and others who deal with precious gems and metals and she will teach these elfin all about the occult and mystical powers of these gems and as well as the spiritual evolution of gems through the ages. These fae come to understand that gems have their own consciousness, powers and destiny and learn how to attune to these for optimal results.

DECEMBER 29TH

Dadynle: Can Feel the Magic

MAGIC: THE CAULDRON OF REBIRTH
CONSTELLATION: OLĖLTRE, TELESCOPIUM
PLANETARY ASSOCIATION: PLUTO
FAERIE ASSISTANTS: LAUKŲ DVASIOS

Dadynle teaches these elfin to become increasingly sensitive to magic, so they can feel spells and cantrips and in time they are able to see their movement and direction, or trace them back to their source. These elfin can also find wells and pools of accumulated and unused magic that others have unwittingly cast off that is free for the taking, like money lying on a sidewalk. Because of their ability to see the course of magic spells, they also develop a certain oracular power, for in seeing the movement of magic they also can divine its probable effects.

NEVER PASS UP AN OPPORTUNITY TO LEARN.
—OLD ELVEN SAYING

The Shining Ones

DECEMBER 30TH
Ridåvyn: Sees to the Heart of Things

MAGIC: THE MAGIC MIRROR
CONSTELLATION: LARCA, LEO
PLANETARY ASSOCIATION: JUPITER
FAERIE ASSISTANTS: AOS SÍ

These fae are evolving the ability to understand situations and individuals very quickly, almost from the first moment they encounter them. There is a danger that in the course of this development they may rely entirely on snap judgments and no longer keep an open mind about things; but as they progress they are able to make quick and accurate appraisals of people and circumstances while simultaneously remaining open to further information for they come to understand that people and events are always in progress and things that seem one way may swing to another way very quickly.

DECEMBER 31ST
Herådyn: Glowing with Magic

MAGIC: THE RINGS OF POWER
CONSTELLATION: DRAKAN, DRACO
PLANETARY ASSOCIATION: ASTEROIDS
FAERIE ASSISTANTS: WATER ELEMENTALS

The elfin under this Shining One's guidance don't do magic so much as radiate magic. Having developed their true S'elves to an advanced degree they can now let the power of their being glow with energetic transformative power and thus influence and affect all around them. The more adept they are in this the less effort they have to use to obtain all that they desire. Things just happen naturally for them, as if by magic. The key to this is an inner feeling of passion, serenity or even realized fantasy that permeates their being and illuminates their surroundings. These fae are becoming very powerful enchanters and come to understand the significance of ambience, attitude and atmosphere.

> *To serve the Shining Ones is to become one of them, for their lives are a continuing example of service.*

> *The elves are under the opinion that people who reject us are usually doing us a favor.*

> *You can't force wisdom to come;*
> *you can just embrace it when it does.*
> *—Old Elven Saying*

> *We are not defined by the Spirits that assist us, but our nature's attract those who are meant for us.*

ABOUT THE AUTHORS

The Silver Elves are a family of elves who have been living and sharing the Elven Way since 1975. They are the authors of *The Book of Elven Runes: A Passage Into Faerie; The Magical Elven Love Letters, volume 1, 2, and 3; An Elfin Book of Spirits: Evoking the Beneficent Powers of Faerie; Caressed by an Elfin Breeze: The Poems of Zardoa Silverstar; Eldafaryn: True Tales of Magic from the Lives of the Silver Elves; Arvyndase (Silverspeech): A Short Course in the Magical Language of the Silver Elves; The Elven Book of Dreams: A Magical Oracle of Faerie; The Book of Elven Magick: The Philosophy and Enchantments of the Seelie Elves, Volume 1 & 2; What An Elf Would Do: A Magical Guide to the Manners and Etiquette of the Faerie Folk; The Elven Tree of Life Eternal: A Magical Quest for One's True S'Elf; Magic Talks: On Being a Correspondence Between the Silver Elves and the Elf Queen's Daughters; Sorcerers' Dialogues: A Further Correspondence Between the Silver Elves and the Founders of the Elf Queen's Daughters; Discourses on High Sorcery: More Correspondence Between the Silver Elves and the Founders of the Elf Queen's Daughters; Ruminations on Necromancy: Continuing Correspondence Between the Silver Elves and the Founders of the Elf Queen's Daughter; The Elven Way: The Magical Path of the Shining Ones; The Book of Elf Names: 5,600 Elven Names to Use for Magic, Game Playing, Inspiration, Naming One's Self and One's Child, and as Words in the Elven Language of the Silver Elves; Elven Silver: The Irreverent Faery Tales of Zardoa Silverstar, An Elven Book of Ryhmes: Book Two of the Magical Poems of Zardoa Silverstar; The Voice of Faerie: Making Any Tarot Deck Into an Elven Oracle; and Liber Aelph: Words of Guidance from the Silver Elves to our Magical Children.*

We have had various articles published in *Circle Network News Magazine* and have given out over 6,000 elven names to interested individuals in the Arvyndase language, with each elf name having a unique meaning specifically for that person. If you wish to know more about us you can read pages 100 to 107 in *Circles, Groves and Sanctuaries*, compiled by Dan and Pauline Campanelli (Llewellyn Publications, 1992), which contains an article by us and photos us and our home/sanctuary as it existed at the time. We are also mentioned numerous times in *Not In Kansas Anymore* by Christine Wicker (Harper San Francisco, 2005), and *A Field Guide to Otherkin* by Lupa (Megalithica Books, 2007). An interview with the Silver Elves is also included in Emily Carding's recent book *Faery Craft.*

The Silver Elves

The Elven Way is the spiritual Path of the Elves. It is not a religion. While all elves are free to pursue whatever spiritual path they desire, or not as the case may be, these elves are magicians and follow no particular religious dogma. We do however believe in all the Gods and Goddesses, (also Santa Claus [to whom we're related], the tooth fairy [distant cousins] and the Easter or Ostara Bunny [no relation].) and try to treat them all with due respect. The Elven Way promotes the principles of Fairness, that is to say both Justice, Elegance and Equal Opportunity and Courtesy that is respectful in its interactions and attitude toward all beings, great or small. We understand the world as a magical or miraculous phenomena, and that all beings, by pursuing their own true path, will become whomever they truly desire to be. Our path is that of Love and Magic and we share our way with all sincerely interested individuals.

If you have any questions about using tarot for wish fulfillment, remember you can always contact us through our website at: http://silverelves.angelfire.com or through our Facebook page, under the name Silver Elves, and we will do our best to help you.

Printed in Great Britain
by Amazon